Books by Edward T. Hall

THE SILENT LANGUAGE

THE HIDDEN DIMENSION

HANDBOOK FOR PROXEMIC RESEARCH

THE FOURTH DIMENSION IN ARCHITECTURE:
The Impact of Building on Man's Behavior
(with Mildred Reed Hall)

THE DANCE OF LIFE:
The Other Dimension of Time

HIDDEN DIFFERENCES:
Doing Business with the Japanese
(with Mildred Reed Hall)

BEYOND CULTURE

THE HIDDEN DIMENSION

The Hidden Dimension

EDWARD T. HALL

ANCHOR BOOKS
DOUBLEDAY
NEW YORK   LONDON   TORONTO   SYDNEY   AUCKLAND

An Anchor Book
PUBLISHED BY DOUBLEDAY
a division of Bantam Doubleday Dell Publishing Group, Inc.
666 Fifth Avenue, New York, New York 10103

ANCHOR BOOKS, DOUBLEDAY, and the portrayal of an anchor
are trademarks of Doubleday, a division of Bantam Doubleday
Dell Publishing Group, Inc.

The Hidden Dimension was originally published in hardcover by
Doubleday in 1966. The Anchor Books edition is
published by arrangement with Doubleday.

All photographs were taken by the author, with the following exceptions:
Plate 1, Sven Gillsäter; Plate 3, H. Hediger; Plate 5, Bud Daley, Chicago *Daily News;* Plate 8, Serge Boutourline; Plate 21, Howard F. Van Zandt; Plate 23, Judith Yonkers; Plate 25, Hedrich-Blessing.

Grateful acknowledgment is made for permission to use excerpts from copyrighted material, as follows:
From *The Painter's Eye* by Maurice Grosser. Copyright © 1951 by Maurice Grosser. Reprinted by permission of Holt, Rinehart and Winston, Inc.
From *Language, Thought, and Reality*, selected writings of Benjamin Lee Whorf, by permission of The M.I.T. Press, Cambridge, Massachusetts. Copyright © 1956, by The Massachusetts Institute of Technology.
From *The Making of the President 1960* by Theodore H. White. Copyright © 1961 by Atheneum House, Inc. Reprinted by permission of the publishers.
From "Prologue: The Birth of Architecture," Copyright © 1965 by W. H. Auden. Reprinted from *About the House*, by W. H. Auden, by permission of Random House, Inc.

Library of Congress Cataloging-in-Publication Data
Hall, Edward Twitchell, 1914–
   The hidden dimension/Edward T. Hall.
     p.   cm.
   Reprint. Originally published: Garden City,
   N.Y.: Doubleday, 1966.
   Includes bibliographical references.
     1. Spatial behavior.   2. Personal space.
     3. Architecture—Psychological aspects.
     4. City planning—Psychological aspects.
   I. Title.
   BF469.H3 1990   90-34870
   304.2′3—dc20   CIP
   ISBN 0-385-08476-5

CONTENTS

AUTHOR'S PREFACE

Generally speaking, two types of books interest the serious reader: those that are content oriented—designed to convey a particular body of knowledge—and those that deal with structure—the way in which events are organized. It is doubtful if an author has any control over which of these two types of books he or she writes, though it is desirable to be aware of the difference. The same applies to the reader whose satisfaction depends largely on unstated expectations. Today, when all of us are overwhelmed with data from many sources, it is easy to understand why people feel that they are losing touch, even in their own field. In spite of television, or possibly because of it, people feel a loss of relatedness to the world at large. Information overload increases the need for organizing frames of reference to integrate the mass of rapidly changing information. *The Hidden Dimension* attempts to provide such an organizing frame for space as a system of communication, and for the spatial aspects of architecture and city planning.

Books of this type, since they are independent of disciplinary lines, are not limited to a particular audience or field. This lack of disciplinary orientation will disappoint readers searching for pat answers and those who wish to find everything classified in terms of content and profession. However, since space relates to everything, it is inevitable that this book would cross disciplinary lines.

In writing about my research on people's use of space—the space that they maintain among themselves and their fellows, and that they build around themselves in their cities, their homes, and their offices—my purpose is to bring to awareness what has been taken for granted. By this means, I hope to increase self-knowledge and decrease alienation. In sum, to help introduce people to themselves.

Regarding the organization of the book, I must mention that as an anthropologist I have made a habit of going back to the beginning and searching out the biological substructures from which human behavior springs. This approach underscores the fact that humankind is first, last, and always a biological organism. The gulf that separates humans from the rest of the animal kingdom is not nearly as great as most people think. Indeed, the more we learn about animals and the intricate adaptation mechanisms evolution has produced, the more relevant these studies become for humans in their search for the solution to many complex human problems.

All of my books deal with the *structure of experience as it is molded by culture*, those deep, common, unstated experiences which members of a given culture share, which they communicate without knowing, and which form the backdrop against which all other events are judged. Knowledge of the cultural dimension as a vast complex of communications on many levels would be virtually unnecessary if it were not for two things: our increasing involvements with people in all parts of the world, and the mixing of subcultures within our own country as people from rural areas and foreign countries pour into our cities.

It is increasingly apparent that clashes between cultural systems are not restricted to international relations. Such clashes are assuming significant proportions within our own country and are exacerbated by the overcrowding in cities. Contrary to popular belief, the many diverse groups that make up our country have proved to be surprisingly persistent in maintaining their separate identities. Superficially, these groups may all look alike and sound somewhat alike, but beneath the surface are manifold unstated, unformulated differences in their structuring of time, space, materials, and relationships. It is these very differences that often result in the distortion of meaning, regardless of good intentions, when peoples of different cultures interact.

As a consequence of writing this book, I have been invited to lecture to hundreds of architectural audiences all over the

United States and to consult on architectural projects. These talks and consultations have been instructive and constitute a body of data on social change. One of my objectives has been to communicate to architects that the spatial experience is not just visual, but *multisensory*. And that people differ in their capacity to visualize—in the quality and intensity of their visual imagery. Some people cannot visualize a house or a room or a garden or a street intersection until after the work has been completed. Architects do not have this problem, which is why they can be architects, but they forget that their clients may lack this ability. A third goal was to establish once and for all that while buildings and towns cannot make up for social injustice, and much more than good city planning is needed to make a democracy work, there is still a close link between mankind and its extensions. No matter what happens in the world of human beings, it happens in a spatial setting, and the design of that setting has a deep and persisting influence on the people in that setting.

My greatest success in promulgating these ideas has been among the younger architects. Bits and pieces of my research have been accepted and applied, but not the organizing frame which includes the idea that everyone receives all information about the environment *through his or her senses*. If one wants to understand the impact of the environment on human beings, it is necessary to know a great deal about the senses and how sensory inputs are handled in the brain.

I have always believed in the importance of aesthetics in architecture, but not at the expense of the people housed in the buildings. Unfortunately, today most buildings communicate in no uncertain terms that designing for people is low on our scale of priorities. All too often architects and planners are hamstrung by decisions made by financial experts concerned with "the bottom line." Financial calculations are seldom based on any understanding of human needs or the ultimate costs of ignoring them.

People need to know that they are important and that architects and planners have their welfare in mind, but it is a rare structure that communicates this basic message. In the context of international relations, it is also important to know that the language of space is just as different as the spoken language. Most important of all, space is one of *the* basic, underlying organizational systems for all living things—particularly for people. Why these statements are true is the subject of this book.

No book reaches a point suitable for publication without the active cooperation and participation of a great many people, all essential. There are always particular members of the team whose roles are more clearly defined and without whose help the manuscript would never have reached the publisher. It is the contribution of these people that I wish to acknowledge.

The first need of authors is for someone to stick with them, to put up with their exasperated impatience when it is pointed out that they have failed to distinguish clearly between what they know and what they have written. For me, writing is something that does not come easily. When I am writing, everything else stops. This means other people must shoulder a heavy burden. My first acknowledgment is, as always, to my wife, Mildred Reed Hall, who is also my partner in my work and who assisted me in my research in so many ways that it is often difficult to separate her contributions from my own.

Support for my research has been generously provided by grants from the National Institute of Mental Health and the Wenner-Gren Foundation for Anthropological Research. I wish to make special mention of a unique institution, the Washington School of Psychiatry. As a Research Fellow of the school and a member of its faculty for many years, I profited enormously from my interaction with its creative work.

The following editors aided me in the production of this manuscript: Roma McNickle; Richard Winslow and Andrea Balchan of Doubleday; and my wife, Mildred Reed Hall. Without their help I could not have produced this volume. I received valuable and loyal assistance from Gudrun Huden and Judith Yonkers, who also provided the line drawings for this book.

I also wish to acknowledge and thank the following for permission to quote: Harcourt, Brace & World for Antoine de St. Exupéry's *Flight to Arras* and *Night Flight;* Harper & Row for Mark Twain's *Captain Stormfield's Visit to Heaven;* Houghton Mifflin for James J. Gibson's *The Perception of the Visual World;* Alfred A. Knopf, Inc., for Franz Kafka's *The Trial* and for Yasunari Kawabata's *Snow Country,* UNESCO Series of Contemporary Works (Japanese Series), translated by Edward G. Seidensticker; *Language* for Edward Sapir's "The Status of Linguistics as a Science"; Massachusetts Institute of Technology for Benjamin Lee Whorf's *Science and Linguistics;* The Technology Press and John Wiley & Sons for Benjamin Lee Whorf's *Language, Thought, and Reality;* the University of Toronto Press for Edmund Carpenter's *Eskimo;* and *The Yale Review,* Yale University Press for Edward S. Deevey's "The Hare and the Haruspex: A Cautionary Tale."

Some of the material in Chapter X appeared previously in my article titled "Silent Assumptions in Social Communication," published in the proceedings of the Association for Research in Nervous and Mental Disease. Permission to use this material is gratefully acknowledged.

THE HIDDEN DIMENSION

I

CULTURE AS COMMUNICATION

The central theme of this book is social and personal space and man's perception of it. Proxemics is the term I have coined for the interrelated observations and theories of man's use of space as a specialized elaboration of culture.

The concepts developed here did not originate with me. Over fifty-three years ago, Franz Boas laid the foundation of the view which I hold that communication constitutes the core of culture and indeed of life itself. In the twenty years that followed, Boas and two other anthropologists, Edward Sapir and Leonard Bloomfield, speakers of the Indo-European languages, were confronted with the radically different languages of the American Indians and the Eskimos. The conflict between these two different language systems produced a revolution concerning the nature of language itself. Before this time, European scholars had taken Indo-European languages as the models for *all* languages. Boas and his followers discovered in effect that each language family is a law unto itself, a closed system, whose patterns the linguist must reveal and describe. It was necessary for the linguistic scientist to consciously avoid the trap of projecting the hidden rules of his own language on to the language being studied.

In the 1930s Benjamin Lee Whorf, a full-time chemist and engineer but an amateur in the field of linguistics, began studying with Sapir. Whorf's papers based on his work with the Hopi and Shawnee Indians had revolutionary implications for the relation of language to both thought and perception. Language, he said, is more than just a medium for expressing thought. It is, in fact, *a major element in the formation of thought*. Furthermore, to use a figure from our own day, man's very perception of the world about him is programmed by the language he speaks, just as a computer is programmed. Like the computer, man's mind will register and structure external reality only in accordance with the program. Since two languages often program the same class of events quite differently, no belief or philosophical system should be considered apart from language.

Only in recent years, and to just a handful of people, have the implications of Whorf's thinking become apparent. Difficult to grasp, they became somewhat frightening when given careful thought. They strike at the root of the doctrine of "free will," because they indicate that all men are captives of the language they speak as long as they take their language for granted.

The thesis of this book and of *The Silent Language,* which preceded it, is that the principles laid down by Whorf and his fellow linguists in relation to language apply to the rest of human behavior as well—in fact, to all culture. It has long been believed that experience is what all men share, that it is always possible somehow to bypass language and culture and to refer back to experience in order to reach another human being. This implicit (and often explicit) belief concerning man's relation to experience was based on the assumptions that, when two human beings are subject to the same "experience," virtually the same data are being fed to the two central nervous systems and that the two brains record similarly.

Proxemic research casts serious doubt on the validity of this assumption, particularly when the cultures are different. Chapters X and XI describe how people from different cultures not only speak different languages but, what is possibly more important, *inhabit different sensory worlds.* Selective screening of sensory data admits some things while filtering out others, so that *experience as it is perceived* through one set of culturally patterned sensory screens is quite different from experience perceived through another. The architectural and urban environments that people create are expressions of this filtering-screening process. In fact, from these man-altered environments, it is possible to learn how different peoples use their senses. Experience, therefore, cannot be counted on as a stable point of reference, because it occurs in a setting that has been molded by man.

The role of the senses in this context is described in Chapters IV through VII. This discussion was included to give the reader some of the basic data on the apparatus man uses in building his perceptual world. Describing the senses in this way is analogous to descriptions of the vocal apparatus as a basis for understanding speech processes.

An examination of how the senses are used by different peoples, as they interact with their living and non-living environment, provides concrete data on some of the differences between, for example, Arabs and Americans. Here at the very source of the interaction it is possible to detect significant variations in what is attended and what is screened out.

My research of the past five years demonstrates that Americans and Arabs live in different sensory worlds much of the time and do not use the same senses even to establish most of the distances maintained during conversations. As we shall see later, Arabs make more use of olfaction and touch than Americans. They interpret their sensory data differently and combine them in different ways. Apparently, even the Arab's experience of the body in its relation to the ego is different from our own. American women who have married Arabs in this country and who have known only the learned American side of their personality have often observed that their husbands assume different personalities when they return to their homelands where they are again immersed in Arab communication and are captives of Arab perceptions. They become in every sense of the word quite different people.

In spite of the fact that cultural systems pattern behavior in radically different ways, they are deeply rooted in biology and physiology. Man is an organism with a wonderful and extraordinary past. He is distinguished from the other animals by virtue of the fact that he has elaborated what I have termed *extensions* of his organism. By developing his extensions, man has been able to improve or specialize various functions. The computer is an extension of part of the brain, the telephone extends the voice, the wheel extends the legs and feet. Language extends experience in time and space while writing extends language. Man has elaborated his extensions to such a degree that we are apt to forget that his humanness is rooted in his animal nature. The anthropologist Weston La Barre has pointed out that man has shifted evolution from his body to his extensions and in so doing has tremendously accelerated the evolutionary process.

Thus any attempt to observe, record, and analyze proxemic systems, which are parts of modern cultures, must take into account the behavioral systems on which they are based as expressed by earlier life forms. Chapters II and III of this book should help to provide both a foundation and a perspective to be used in considering the more complex human elaborations of space behavior in animals. Much of the thinking and interpretation of data that went into this book has been influenced by the tremendous strides made in recent years by ethologists, the scientists who study animal behavior and the relation of organisms to their environment.

In light of what is known of ethology, it may be profitable in the long run if man is viewed as an organism that has elaborated and specialized his extensions to such a degree that they have taken over, and are rapidly replacing, nature. In other words, man has created a new dimension, the cultural dimension, of which proxemics is only a part. The relationship between man and the cultural dimension is one in which both *man and his environment participate in molding each other*. Man is now in the position of actually creating the total world in which he lives, what the ethologists refer to as his biotope. In creating this world he is actually determining *what kind of an organism* he will be. This is a frightening thought in view of how very little is known about man. It also means that, in a very deep sense, our cities are creating different types of people in their slums, mental hospitals, prisons, and suburbs. These subtle interactions make the problems of urban renewal and the integration of minorities into the dominant culture more difficult than is often anticipated. Similarly, our lack of full understanding of the relation of peoples *and* their biotope is compounding the process of technical development of the so-called underdeveloped nations of the world.

What happens when people of different cultures meet and become involved? In *The Silent Language* I suggested that communication occurs simultaneously on different levels of consciousness, ranging from full awareness to out-of-awareness. Recently it has become necessary to expand this view. When people communicate they do much more than just toss the conversational ball back and forth. My own studies as well as those of others reveal a series of delicately controlled, culturally conditioned servomechanisms that keeps life on an even keel, much like the automatic pilot on the airplane. All of us are sensitive to subtle changes in the demeanor of the other person as he responds to what we are saying or doing. In most situations people will at first unconsciously and later consciously avoid escalation of what I have termed the adumbrative or foreshadowing part of a communication from the barely perceptible signs of annoyance to open hostility. In the animal world, if the adumbrative process is short-circuited or bypassed, vicious fighting is apt to occur. In humans in the international-intercultural sphere of life many difficulties can be traced to failure to read adumbrations correctly. In such instances, by the time people discover what is going on, they are so deeply involved that they can't back out.

The following chapters include many instances of the thwarting of communication primarily because neither of the parties was aware that each inhabits a different perceptual world. Each was also interpreting the other's spoken words in a context that included both behavior and setting, with a result that positive reinforcement of friendly overtures was often random or even absent.

Indeed, it is now believed by ethologists such as Konrad Lorenz that aggression is a necessary ingredient of life; without it, life as we know it would probably not be possible. Normally, aggression leads to proper spacing of animals, lest they become so numerous as to destroy their environment and themselves along with it. When crowding becomes too great after population buildups, interactions intensify, leading to greater and greater stress. As psychological and emotional stress builds up and tempers wear thin, subtle but powerful changes occur in the chemistry of the body. Births drop while deaths progressively increase until a state known as population collapse occurs. Such cycles of buildup and collapse are now generally recognized as normal for the warm-blooded vertebrates and possibly for all life. Contrary to popular belief, the food supply is only indirectly involved in these cycles, as demonstrated by John Christian and V. C. Wynne-Edwards. As man developed culture he domesticated himself and in the process created a whole new series of worlds, each different from the other. Each world has its own set of sensory inputs, so that what crowds people of one culture does not necessarily crowd another. Similarly, an act that releases aggression and would therefore be stressful to one people may be neutral to the next. Nevertheless, it is fairly obvious that the American Negroes and people of Spanish culture who are flocking to our cities are being very seriously stressed. Not only are they in a setting that does not fit them, but they have passed the limits of their own tolerance to stress. The United States is faced with the fact that two of its creative and sensitive peoples are in the process of being destroyed and like Samson could bring down the structure that houses us all. Thus it must be impressed upon architects, city planners, and builders that if this country is to avoid catastrophe, we must begin seeing man as an interlocutor with his environment, an environment which these same planners, architects, and builders are now creating with little reference to man's proxemic needs.

To those of us who produce the income and pay the taxes which support government, I say that whatever the cost of rebuilding our cities, this cost will have to be met if America is to survive. Most important, the rebuilding of our cities must be based upon research which leads to an understanding of man's needs and a knowledge of the many sensory worlds of the different groups of people who inhabit American cities.

The chapters that follow are intended to convey a basic message about the nature of man and his relationship to his environment. The message is this:

There is a great need to revise and broaden our view of the human situation, a need to be both more comprehensive and more realistic, not only about others, but about ourselves as well. It is essential that we learn to read the silent communications as easily as the printed and spoken ones. Only by doing so can we also reach other people, both inside and outside our national boundaries, as we are increasingly required to do.

II

DISTANCE REGULATION IN ANIMALS

Comparative studies of animals help to show how man's space requirements are influenced by his environment. In animals we can observe the direction, the rate, and the extent of changes in behavior that follow changes in space available to them as we can never hope to do in men. For one thing, by using animals it is possible to accelerate time, since animal generations are relatively short. A scientist can, in forty years, observe four hundred forty generations of mice, while he has in the same span of time seen only two generations of his own kind. And, of course, he can be more detached about the fate of animals.

In addition, animals don't rationalize their behavior and thus obscure issues. In their natural state, they respond in an amazingly consistent manner so that it is possible to observe repeated and virtually identical performances. By restricting our observations to the way animals handle space, it is possible to learn an amazing amount that is translatable to human terms.

Territoriality, a basic concept in the study of animal behavior, is usually defined as behavior by which an organism characteristically lays claim to an area and defends it against members of its own species. It is a recent concept, first described by the English ornithologist H. E. Howard in his *Territory in Bird Life*, written in 1920. Howard stated the concept in some detail, though naturalists as far back as the seventeenth century had taken note of various events which Howard recognized as manifestations of territoriality.

Territoriality studies are already revising many of our basic ideas of animal life and human life as well. The expression "free as a bird" is an encapsulated form of man's conception of his relation to nature. He sees animals as free to roam the world, while he himself is imprisoned by society. Studies of territoriality show that the reverse is closer to the truth and that animals are often imprisoned in their own territories. It is doubtful if Freud, had he known what is known today about the relation of animals to space, could have attributed man's advances to trapped energy redirected by culturally imposed inhibitions.

Many important functions are expressed in territoriality, and new ones are constantly being discovered. H. Hediger, Zurich's famous animal psychologist, described the most important aspects of territoriality and explained succinctly the mechanisms by which it operates. Territoriality, he says, insures the propagation of the species by regulating density. It provides a frame in which things are done—places to learn, places to play, safe places to hide. Thus it co-ordinates the activities of the group and holds the group together. It keeps animals within communicating distance of each other, so that the presence of food or an enemy can be signaled. An animal with a territory of its own can develop an inventory of reflex responses to terrain features. When danger strikes, the animal on its home ground can take advantage of automatic responses rather than having to take time to think about where to hide.

The psychologist C. R. Carpenter, who pioneered in the observation of monkeys in a native setting, listed thirty-two functions of territoriality, including important ones relating to the protection and evolution of the species. The list that follows is not complete, nor is it representative of all species, but it indicates the crucial nature of territoriality as a behavioral system, *a system that evolved in very much the same way as anatomical systems evolved.* In fact, differences in territoriality have become so widely recognized that they are used as a basis for distinguishing between species, much as anatomical features are used.

Territoriality offers protection from predators, and also exposes to predation the unfit who are too weak to establish and defend a territory. Thus, it reinforces dominance in selective breeding because the less dominant animals are less likely to establish territories. On the other hand territoriality facilitates breeding by providing a home base that is safe. It aids in protecting the nests and the young in them. In some species it localizes waste disposal and inhibits or prevents parasites. Yet one of the most important functions of territoriality is proper spacing, which protects against overexploitation of that part of the environment on which a species depends for its living.

In addition to preservation of the species and the environment, personal and social functions are associated with territoriality. C. R. Carpenter tested the relative roles of sexual vigor and dominance in a territorial context and found that even a desexed pigeon will in its own territory regularly win a test encounter with a normal male, even though desexing usually results in loss of position in a social hierarchy. Thus, while dominant animals determine the general direction in which the species develops, the fact that the subordinate can win (and so breed) on his home grounds helps to preserve plasticity in the species by increasing variety and thus preventing the dominant animals from freezing the direction which evolution takes.

Territoriality is also associated with status. A series of experiments by the British ornithologist A. D. Bain on the great tit altered and even reversed dominance relationships by shifting the position of feeding stations in relation to birds living in adjacent areas. As the feeding station was placed closer and closer to a bird's home range, the bird would accrue advantages it lacked when away from its own home ground.

Man, too, has territoriality and he has invented many ways of defending what he considers his own land, turf, or spread. The removal of boundary markers and trespass upon the property of another man are punishable acts in much of the Western world. A man's home has been his castle in English common law for centuries, and it is protected by prohibitions on unlawful search and seizure even by officials of his government. The

distinction is carefully made between private property, which is the territory of an individual, and public property, which is the territory of the group.

This cursory review of the functions of territoriality should suffice to establish the fact that it is a basic behavioral system characteristic of living organisms including man.

SPACING MECHANISMS IN ANIMALS

In addition to territory that is identified with a particular plot of ground, each animal is surrounded by a series of bubbles or irregularly shaped balloons that serve to maintain proper spacing between individuals. Hediger has identified and described a number of such distances which appear to be used in one form or another by most animals. Two of these —flight distance and critical distance—are used when individuals of *different species meet;* whereas personal distance and social distance can be observed during interactions between members of the same species.

Flight Distance

Any observant person has noticed that a wild animal will allow a man or other potential enemy to approach only up to a given distance before it flees. "Flight distance" is Hediger's term for this interspecies spacing mechanism. As a general rule, there is a positive correlation between the size of an animal and its flight distance—the larger the animal, the greater the distance it must keep between itself and the enemy. An antelope will flee when the intruder is as much as five hundred yards away. The wall lizard's flight distance, on the other hand, is about six feet.

There are, of course, other ways of coping with a predator, such as camouflage, protective armor or spines, or offensive odor. But flight is the basic mechanism of survival for mobile creatures. In domesticating other animals, man has had to eliminate or radically reduce the flight reaction. In zoos, it is essential to modify the flight reaction enough so that the captive animal can move about, sleep, and eat without being panicked by man.

Although man is a self-domesticated animal, the domestication process is only partial. We see this in certain types of schizophrenics who apparently experience something very similar to the flight reaction. When approached too closely, these schizophrenics panic in much the same way as an animal recently locked up in a zoo. In describing their feelings, such patients refer to anything that happens within their "flight distance" as taking place literally *inside themselves*. That is, the boundaries of the self extend beyond the body. These experiences recorded by therapists working with schizophrenics indicate that the realization of the self as we know it is intimately associated with the process of making boundaries explicit. This same relationship between boundaries and self can also be observed in cross-cultural contexts, as we shall see in Chapter XI.

Critical Distance

Critical distances or zones apparently are present wherever and whenever there is a flight reaction. "Critical distance" encompasses the narrow zone separating flight distance from attack distance. A lion in a zoo will flee from an approaching man until it meets an insurmountable barrier. If the man continues the approach, he soon penetrates the lion's critical distance, at which point the cornered lion reverses direction and begins slowly to stalk the man.

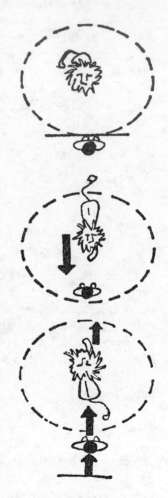

In the classical animal act in the circus, the lion's stalking is so deliberate that he will surmount an intervening obstacle such as a stool in order to get at the man. To get the lion to remain on the stool, the lion tamer quickly steps out of the critical zone. At this point, the lion stops pursuing. The trainer's elaborate "protective" devices—the chair, the whip, or the gun—are so much window dressing. Hediger says the critical distance for the animals he has knowledge of is so precise that it can be measured in centimeters.

Contact and Non-Contact Species

In regard to the use of space, it is possible to observe a basic and sometimes inexplicable dichotomy in the animal world. Some species huddle together and require physical contact with each other. Others completely avoid touching. No apparent logic governs the category into which a species falls. Contact creatures include the walrus, the hippopotamus, the pig, the brown bat, the parakeet, and the hedgehog among many other species. The horse, the dog, the cat, the rat, the muskrat, the hawk, and the blackheaded gull are non-contact species. Curiously enough, closely related animals may belong to different categories. The great Emperor penguin is a contact species. It conserves heat through contact with its fellows by huddling together in large groups and thus increases its adaptability to cold. Its range extends over many parts of Antarctica. The smaller Adelie penguin is a non-contact species. Thus it is somewhat less adaptable to cold than the Emperor, and its range is apparently more limited.

What other functions may be served by contact behavior are unknown. One could hazard a guess that, since contact animals are more "involved" with each other, their social organization and possibly their manner of exploiting the environment might be different from those of non-contact animals. Non-contact species, one would think, would be more vulnerable to the stresses exerted by crowding. It is clear that all warm-blooded animals begin life in the contact phase. This phase is only temporary with the many non-contact species, for the young abandon it as soon as they leave their parents and are on their own. From this point in the life cycle of both types, regular spacing between individuals can be observed.

Personal Distance

Personal distance is the term applied by Hediger to the normal spacing that non-contact animals maintain between themselves and their fellows. This distance acts as an invisible bubble that surrounds the organism. Outside the bubble two organisms are not as intimately involved with each other as when the bubbles overlap. Social organization is a factor in personal distance. Dominant animals tend to have larger personal distances than those which occupy lower positions in the social hierarchy, while subordinate animals have been observed to yield room to dominant ones. Glen McBride, an Australian professor of animal husbandry, has made detailed observations of the spacing of domestic fowl as a function of dominance. His theory of "social organization and behavior" has as a main element the handling of space. This correlation of personal distance and status in one form or another seems to occur throughout the vertebrate kingdom. It has been reported for birds and many mammals, including the colony of ground-living Old World monkeys at the Japanese Monkey Center near Nagoya.

Aggression is an essential component in the make-up of vertebrates. A strong, aggressive animal can eliminate weaker rivals. There seems to be a relation between aggression and display so that the more aggressive animals display more vigorously. In this way, too, display and aggression serve as handmaidens in the process of natural selection. To insure survival of the species, however, aggression must be regulated. This can be done in two ways: by development of hierarchies and by spacing. Ethologists seem to agree that spacing is the more primitive method, not only because it is the simplest but because it is less flexible.

Social Distance

Social animals need to stay in touch with each other. Loss of contact with the group can be fatal for a variety of reasons including exposure to predators. Social distance is not simply the distance at which an animal will lose contact with his group—that is, the distance at which it can no longer see, hear, or smell the group—it is rather a psychological distance, one at which the animal apparently begins to feel anxious when he exceeds its limits. We can think of it as a hidden band that *contains* the group.

Social distance varies from species to species. It is quite short—apparently only a few yards—among flamingos, and quite long among some other birds. The late E. Thomas Gilliard, an American ornithologist, tells how clans of male bowerbirds maintain contact "over many thousands of feet by means of mighty whistles and harsh, rasping notes."

Social distance is not always rigidly fixed but is determined in part by the situation. When the young of apes and humans are mobile but not yet under control of the mother's voice, social distance may be the length of her reach. This is readily observed among the baboons in a zoo. When the baby approaches a certain point, the mother reaches out to seize the end of its tail and pull it back to her. When added control is needed because of danger, social distance shrinks. To document this in man, one has only to watch a family with a number of small children holding hands as they cross a busy street.

Social distance in man has been extended by telephone, TV, and the walkie-talkie, making it possible to integrate the activities of groups over great distances. Increased social distance is now remaking social and political institutions in ways that have only recently begun to be studied.

POPULATION CONTROL

In the cold waters of the North Sea lives a form of crab, *Hyas araneus*. The distinguishing feature of the species is that, at certain times in the life cycle, the individual becomes vulnerable to others of the same species, and some are sacrificed to keep the population down. Periodically, when the crab sheds its shell, its only protection is the space that separates it from crabs in the hard-shell stage. Once a hard-shelled crab gets close enough to scent his soft-shelled fellow—that is, once the olfactory boundary is passed—smell leads the hard-shelled predator to his next meal.

Hyas araneus provides us with an example of both a "critical space" and a "critical situation." These terms were originally used by Wilhelm Schäfer, Director of the Frankfurt Natural History Museum. Schäfer, in an attempt to understand basic life processes, was one of the first to examine the ways in which organisms handle space. His 1956 study was unique in directing attention to crises of survival. Animal societies, he stated, build up until a critical density is reached, thus creating a crisis that must be met if the society is to survive. Schäfer's important contribution was to classify crises of survival and find a pattern in the various ways which simple forms of life have worked out to deal with the crowding that brings on such crises. Schäfer analyzed the process that relates population control to the solution of other important life problems.

As we have already seen, all animals have a minimum space requirement, without which survival is impossible. This is the "critical space" of the organism. When the population has built up so greatly that the critical space is no longer available, a "critical situation" develops. The simplest way of handling the situation is to remove some individuals. This can be accomplished in a variety of ways, one of which is illustrated by *Hyas araneus*.

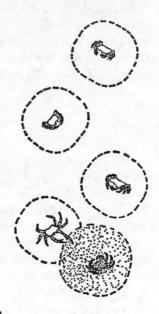

Crabs are solitary animals. At the time in the life cycle when they must locate other crabs in order to reproduce, they find each other by smell. Thus the survival of the species depends on not having individuals roam so far apart that they cannot smell each other. But the critical space crabs need is also well defined. When their numbers increase to the point where critical space is not available, enough of those individuals who are in the soft-shell stage are eaten to bring the population back to a level at which individuals have enough room.

THE STICKLEBACK SEQUENCE

Several notches above the crab on the evolutionary scale is the stickleback, a small fish that is common in shallow fresh waters in Europe. The stickleback was made famous when the Dutch ethologist Niko Tinbergen identified the complex sequence the fish has developed to reproduce itself. Tinbergen later showed that a short-circuiting of the sequence results in a population decrease.

In the spring, each male stickleback carves out a circular territory, defends it several times against all comers, and builds a nest. His inconspicuous gray coloring then changes, so that his chin and belly are bright red, his back blue-white, and his eyes blue. The change in coloration serves to attract females and repel males.

When a female, her belly swollen with eggs, comes within range of the stickleback's nest, the male zigzags toward her, alternately displaying his face and colorful profile. The two-step approach ceremony must be repeated several times before the female will follow the male and enter the nest. Shifting from the visual mode of communication to the more basic one of touch, the male with his nose rhythmically prods the female at the base of her spine until she lays her eggs. The male then enters the nest, fertilizes the eggs, and drives the female away. He repeats this sequence until four or five females have deposited eggs in his nest.

At this point the mating impulse subsides, and a new set of responses is observed. The male becomes his old inconspicuous gray. His role now is to defend the nest and keep the eggs supplied with oxygen by fanning water through the nest with his pectoral fins. When the eggs hatch, the male protects the young fish until they are big enough to fend for themselves. He will even catch those that wander too far, carrying them in his mouth carefully back to the nest.

The stickleback's behavior sequence—including fighting, mating, and caring for the young—is so predictable that Tinbergen was able to conduct a series of experiments which provides valuable insights into the message systems or signals that release responses to the different drives. The male's zigzag approach to the female is a response to an urge to attack, which has to run its course before the sexual urge takes over. The swollen shape of the egg-heavy female releases the courting response in the male. After she has laid her eggs, red no longer attracts her. She will not lay eggs until she has been prodded by the male. Thus, vision and touch trigger the several elements of the sequence.

The predictable nature of the sequence enabled Tinbergen to observe in experimental situations what happens when the sequence is interrupted by the presence of too many males and consequent crowding of individual territories. The red of too many males disrupts courting. Some steps in the sequence are omitted so that eggs are not laid in a nest or fertilized. Under very crowded conditions, males will battle each other until some are killed.

MALTHUS RECONSIDERED

The crab and the stickleback provide useful information about the relation of space to reproduction and population control. The crab's sense of smell is the key to distance required by the individual and determines the maximum number of crabs that can inhabit a given area of the sea. In the stickleback, sight and touch set off an ordered sequence that must run its course if the fish is to reproduce. Crowding disrupts this sequence and thus interferes with reproduction. In both animals acuity of the receptors—smell, sight, touch, or a combination—determines the distance at which individuals can live and continue to perform the reproduction cycle. Without proper maintenance of this distance, they lose the battle to one of their own kind, rather than to starvation, disease, or a predator.

There is a growing need for reconsideration of the Malthusian doctrine which relates population to the food supply. For centuries, Scandinavians have watched the march of the lemmings to the sea. Similar suicidal activities have been observed among rabbits at the time of large-scale population buildups followed by die-off. Natives of certain Pacific islands have seen rats doing the same sort of thing. This weird behavior on the part of certain animals has led to every imaginable explanation, yet it wasn't until recently that some insight was gained as to the factors that lay behind the lemmings' mad dash.

About the time of World War II, a few scientists began

to suspect that there was more to population control than predators and food supply and that the behavior of lemmings and rabbits might bear on these other factors. At the time of large-scale die-offs, there appeared to be plenty of food available, and carcasses showed no signs of starvation.

Among the scientists studying this phenomenon was John Christian, an ethologist with training in medical pathology. In 1950 he advanced the thesis that increase and decrease in mammalian populations are controlled by physiological mechanisms that respond to *density*. He presented evidence showing that as numbers of animals in a given area increase, stress builds up until it triggers an endocrine reaction that acts to collapse the population.

Christian needed more data and had been looking for a chance to study a mammalian population in the actual process of collapsing. The ideal situation would be one in which endocrine studies could be made before, during, and after collapse. Fortunately, the buildup of the population of the James Island deer came to his attention before it was too late.

THE DIE-OFF ON JAMES ISLAND

About fourteen miles west of the town of Cambridge, Maryland, and less than a mile out in Chesapeake Bay lies James Island, approximately half a square mile (280 acres) of uninhabited land. In 1916 four or five Sika deer (*Cervus nippon*) were released on the island. Breeding freely, the herd built up steadily until it numbered between 280 and 300, a density of about one deer per acre. At this point, reached in 1955, it was apparent that something would have to give before too long.

In 1955, Christian began his research by shooting five deer for detailed histological studies of the adrenal glands, thymus, spleen, thyroid, gonads, kidneys, liver, heart, lungs, and other tissues. The deer were weighed, the contents of their stomachs recorded, and age, sex, and general condition, as well as the presence or absence of deposits of fat under the skin, in the abdomen, and between the muscles, were noted.

Once these records were made, the observers settled down

to wait. In 1956 and 1957 no change occurred. But in the first three months of 1958, over half of the deer died, and 161 carcasses were recovered. The following year more deer died and another drop took place. The population stabilized at around eighty. Twelve deer were collected for histological study between March 1958 and March 1960.

What was responsible for the sudden death of one hundred ninety deer in a two-year period? It wasn't starvation, because the food supply was adequate. In fact, all of the deer collected were in excellent condition, with shining coats, well-developed muscles, and fat deposits between the muscles.

Carcasses collected between 1959 and 1960 resembled those taken in 1956 and 1957 in every outward respect but one. The deer taken after the population collapse and stabilization were markedly larger in body size than those taken just before and during the die-off. The 1960 bucks averaged 34 per cent heavier than the 1958 bucks. Does taken in 1960 were 28 per cent heavier than the 1955–57 does.

The weight of the adrenal glands of the Sika deer remained constant from 1955 to 1958, during the period of maximum density and die-off. The weight decreased 46 per cent between 1958 and 1960. In immature deer, who formed a large proportion of the casualties, adrenal weight dropped 81 per cent after the die-off. There were also important changes in the cell structure of the adrenals that pointed to great stress, even in the survivors. While two cases of hepatitis were discovered, it was thought that these were a result of decreased resistance to stress due to overactive adrenals. In interpreting Christian's data, it is important to clarify the significance of the adrenal glands. The adrenals play an important part in the regulation of growth, reproduction, and the level of the body's defenses. The size and weight of these important glands is not fixed but responds to stress. When animals are too frequently stressed, the adrenals, in order to meet the emergency, become overactive and enlarged. The enlarged adrenals of characteristic cell structure showing stress were therefore highly significant.

An added factor which undoubtedly contributed to stress was the fact that freezing weather in February of 1958 prevented the deer from swimming to the mainland at night, as was their custom, a journey which afforded at least temporary respite from crowding. The major die-off followed this freeze. Lack of relief from confinement, combined with cold, which is also known to cause stress, may have been the last straw.

Summing up at a symposium on crowding, stress, and natural selection in 1961, Christian stated: "Mortality evidently resulted from shock following severe metabolic disturbance, probably as a result of prolonged adrenocortical hyperactivity, judging from the histological material. There was no evidence of infection, starvation, or other obvious cause to explain the mass mortality."

From the physiological side, Christian's study is complete and leaves nothing to be desired. There are, however, some questions about the behavior of the deer under stress that will remain unanswered until another opportunity presents itself. For example, did they show increased aggression? Was this one reason why about nine-tenths of the casualties during the die-off were does and fawns? Hopefully, it will be possible to have a year-round observer next time.

PREDATION AND POPULATION

Less dramatic, but useful in supplying additional evidence that the Malthusian doctrine cannot account for the majority of mass die-offs, were the late Paul Errington's investigations of predation. Errington found, on examining the stomach contents of owls, that a very high proportion consisted of young, immature, old, or sick animals (which were too slow to escape the predator). In a study of muskrats, he found that more died of disease, apparently as a consequence of lowered resistance due to stress from overcrowding, than were captured by the voracious mink. Twice in one year, muskrats dead of disease were found in one lodge. Errington states that muskrats share with men the propensity of growing savage under stress from crowding. He also shows that crowding past a certain limit results in lowered birth rates for muskrats.

By now, many ethologists have on their own come to the conclusion that the relationship of the predator to his prey is one of subtle symbiosis in which the predator does not control population but is rather a constant environmental pressure that acts to improve the species. Interestingly enough, little attention is paid to these studies. A recent example has been described in detail by the biologist Farley Mowat, who was sent to the Arctic by the Canadian government to establish the number of caribou killed by wolves. The caribou herds have been dwindling so that the wolves could be exterminated in clear conscience. He found that: (a) the wolves accounted for only a small number of caribou deaths; (b) they were important to the caribou in keeping the herds healthy and strong (a fact which the Eskimo knew all along); and (c) it was the killing of caribou by *hunters and trappers* to feed their dogs in the winter which was decreasing the herds. In spite of the convincing, carefully marshaled evidence which appears in his book, *Never Cry Wolf,* wolves are now being systematically poisoned, according to Mowat. While it is not possible to calculate in advance what the loss of the Arctic wolf will mean, the lesson should not be ignored. This is simply one of the many examples of how shortsighted cupidity can threaten the balance of nature. When the wolves are gone, the caribou will continue to decrease because the hunters will be there. Those that remain will not be kept as strong as before due to removal of the therapeutic pressure formerly provided by the wolves.

The above examples fall into the general category of the natural experiment. What happens when an element of control is introduced and populations of animals are allowed to build up freely with plenty of food but in the absence of predators? The experiments and studies described in the next chapter reveal quite clearly that predation and food supply may be less significant than we think. They document in detail the role of stress from crowding as a factor in population control and provide some insights into the biochemical mechanisms of population control.

III

CROWDING AND SOCIAL BEHAVIOR IN ANIMALS

CALHOUN'S EXPERIMENTS

Anyone driving along a country road outside Rockville, Maryland, in 1958 would hardly have noticed an ordinary stone barn set back from the road. Inside it was far from ordinary, however, for it housed a structure set up by the ethologist John Calhoun to provide for the material needs of several colonies of domesticated white Norway rats. Calhoun wished to create a situation in which it would be possible to observe the behavior of the rat colonies at any time.

Actually, the experiments in the barn represented only the most recent phase of a fourteen-year research program. In March 1947, Calhoun initiated his studies of population dynamics under natural conditions by introducing five pregnant *wild* Norway rats into a quarter-acre outdoor pen. His observations covered twenty-eight months. Even with plenty of food and no pressure from predation, the population never exceeded 200 individuals, and stabilized at 150. The difference between experiments carried out in the laboratory and what happens to wild rats living under more natural conditions is emphasized by these studies. Calhoun makes the point that in the twenty-eight months covered by the study the five female rats could have produced 50,000 progeny. Yet available space could not have accommodated this number. Nevertheless 5000 rats can be kept in a healthy state in 10,000 square feet of space if they are kept in pens two feet square. If the cage size is reduced to eight inches, the 50,000 rats can not only be accommodated but remain healthy. The question

Calhoun posed was, Why did the population level off at 150 in the wild state?

Calhoun discovered that even with 150 rats in a quarter-acre pen fighting was so disruptive to normal maternal care that only a few of the young survived. Furthermore, the rats were not randomly scattered throughout the area, but had organized themselves into twelve or thirteen discrete local colonies of a dozen rats each. He also noted that twelve rats is the maximum number that can live harmoniously in a natural group and that even this number may induce stress with all the physiological side effects described at the end of Chapter II.

The experience gained with the outdoor pen enabled Calhoun to design a set of experiments in which rat populations could build up freely under conditions that would permit detailed observation without influencing the behavior of the rats in relation to each other.

The results of these experiments are sufficiently startling to warrant a detailed description. Alone, they tell us a great deal about how organisms behave under different conditions of crowding, and they throw new light on how the social behavior that accompanies crowding can have significant physiological consequences. Combined with Christian's work mentioned earlier and with hundreds of other experiments and observations on animals ranging from weasels and mice to humans, Calhoun's studies take on added significance.

Calhoun's experiments are unusual because psychologists conducting this type of research traditionally attempt to control or eliminate all except one or two variables which they can then manipulate at will. Also most of their research applies to the responses of individual organisms. Calhoun's experiments, however, dealt with large, reasonably complex groups. By choosing subjects with a short life span, he was able to correct a defect common to group behavior studies —that they usually cover too little time, and thus fail to show the accumulation effect of a given set of circumstances on several generations. Calhoun's methods were in the best tradition of science. Not content with simply one or two sixteen-month runs in which the population was allowed to build up, he ran six, beginning in 1958 and ending in 1961. The findings of these studies are so varied and so broad in their implications that it is difficult to do justice to them. They should continue to produce new insight for years to come.

Design of the Experiment

Inside his Rockville barn, Calhoun built three 10 by 14-foot rooms open to observation through 3 by 5-foot glass windows cut in the floor of the hayloft. This arrangement permitted observers to have a complete view of the lighted room at any time of the day or night without disturbing the rat. Each room was divided into four pens by electrified partitions. Each pen was a complete dwelling unit, containing a food hopper, a drinking trough, places to nest (skyscraper type burrows for observation), and nesting materials. Ramps over the electrified fence connected all pens but I and IV. These areas then became the end pens of a row of four that had been folded to save space.

The experience with the wild rats had indicated that forty to forty-eight rats could occupy the room. If they were equally divided, each pen would accommodate a colony of twelve rats, the maximum number of a normal group before serious stress from crowding occurs.

To begin his studies, Calhoun placed one or two pregnant females about to give birth in each pen with ramps removed, and allowed the young to mature. A balanced sex ratio was maintained by removing the excess so that his first series began with thirty-two rats, offspring of the five females. Then ramps were replaced and all rats were allowed complete freedom to explore all four pens. The second series began with fifty-six rats, and the mothers were removed upon weaning their young. As in the first series, the connecting ramps were replaced so that the young mature rats could explore all four pens.

From this point on, human intervention ceased except for the removal of surplus infants. This was done in order to prevent the population from exceeding a limit of eighty, twice that at which stress was definitely detectable. Calhoun reasoned that if he failed to maintain this safety margin, the colonies would suffer a population collapse, or die-off, similar to that of the Sika deer, from which they would not recover. His strategy was to maintain a population in a stressful situation while three generations of rats were reared, so that he could study the effects of stress not only on individuals but on several generations.

Development of the Sink

The word "sink" is used figuratively to mean a receptacle of foul or waste things. Calhoun invented the term "behavioral sink" to designate the gross distortions of behavior which appeared among the majority of the rats in the Rockville barn. Such a phenomenon, he believes, is "the outcome of any behavioral process that collects animals together in unusually great numbers. The unhealthy connotations of the term are not accidental: a behavioral sink does act to aggravate all forms of pathology that can be found within a group."

The behavioral sink included disruptions of nest building, courting, sex behavior, reproduction, and social organization. Autopsied rats showed serious physiological effects as well.

The sink was reached when the population density was approximately double that which had been observed to produce a maximum of stress in the wild rat colony. The term "density" must be expanded beyond simple ratio of individuals to available space. Except in the most extreme cases, density alone seldom causes stress in animals.

In order to grasp Calhoun's idea, we need to move for the moment to the young rats and follow them from the time they were given freedom to roam the four pens to the time when the sink developed. In the normal uncrowded state, there is a short period when the young but physically mature male rats fight with each other until they establish a fairly stable social hierarchy. In the first of the two Rockville series described here, two dominant male rats established territories in Pens I and IV. Each maintained a harem of eight to ten females, so that his colony was balanced and consistent with the natu-

ral grouping among rats as observed in the
quarter-acre pen. The remaining fourteen
male rats distributed themselves in Pens II
and III. As the population built up to sixty
or more, the chances of a rat's being able to
eat by himself were minimal. This was because food hoppers had been so designed that
food pellets behind a wire screen took a
long time to extract. The rats in Pens II and
III became conditioned, therefore, to eating
with other rats. Calhoun's observations revealed that *when activity built up in the
middle pens so that the food hoppers were
used from three to five times more frequently
than the end pens, the sink began to develop.*
Normal patterns of behavior were disrupted as follows.

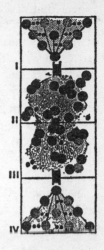

Courting and Sex

Courting and sex in the Norway rat normally involve a
fixed sequence of events. Male rats have to be able to make
three basic distinctions in the selection of a mate. First, they
have to make the usual male-female distinction and be able
to tell the difference between mature and immature individuals. Then they must find a female in a receptive (oestrous)
state. When this combination appears within his visual and
olfactory field, the male rat chases the female. She runs, but
not too fast, and ducks down into the burrow, turns around
and sticks her head up to watch the male. He runs around the
opening of the burrow and performs a little dance. When
the dance is over, the female leaves the burrow and mounting
takes place. During the sex act, the male will grasp the skin
on the female's neck gently between his teeth.

When the sink developed in Pens II and III, everything
changed. Several different categories of males could be
identified:

1. The aggressively dominant, of whom there might be as
many as three, exhibited normal behavior.
2. The passive males avoided both fighting and sex.

3. The hyperactive subordinate males spent their time chasing females. Three or four might be tailing one harassed female at the same time. During the pursuit phase, they would fail to observe the amenities; instead of stopping at the "burrow" entrance they would follow the female inside so that she had no respite. During mounting, these male rats frequently maintained their grasp on females for several minutes instead of the usual two or three seconds.

4. Pansexual males tried mounting anything; receptive and non-receptive females, males and females alike, young and old. Any sex partner would do.

5. Some males withdrew from social and sexual intercourse and went abroad chiefly at the time when other rats slept.

Nest Building

Both male and female rats participate in building but the female does most of the work. Nesting material is carried into the burrow, piled up, and hollowed out to form a cavity to hold the young. In the Rockville study, females from the "harems" in Pens I and IV and others who had not reached the sink stage were "good housekeepers"; they were neat and kept the area around the nest picked up. Sink females in II and III often failed to complete the nest. They could be seen carrying a piece of nesting material up a ramp and suddenly dropping it. Material that reached the nest was either dropped in the general area or added to a pile that was never hollowed out, so that the young became scattered at birth and few survived.

Care of the Young

Normally, females work hard to keep litters sorted out and if a strange pup was introduced into the nest, the female would remove it. When nests were uncovered, the young would be moved to a new location that was more protected. Sink mothers in the Rockville study failed to sort out the young. Litters became mixed; the young were stepped on and often eaten by hyperactive males who invaded the nests. When a nest was exposed, the mother would start moving the young but would fail to complete some phase of the move. Young carried outside to another nest were often dropped and eaten by other rats.

Territoriality and Social Organization

The Norway rat has evolved a simple social organizational pattern that calls for living in groups of ten to twelve hierarchically graded individuals occupying a common territory which they defend. The group is dominated by one mature male and is made up of varying proportions of both sexes. High-ranking rats do not have to defer to other rats as much as low-ranking rats. Their status is indicated in part by those areas within the territory which are open to them. The higher the status, the greater the number of areas they may visit.

Dominant male rats in the sink, unable to establish territories, substituted time for space. Three times daily there was a tempestuous "changing of the guard" around the eating bins that was characterized by fighting and scuffling. Each group was dominated by a single male. These three males were equal to each other in rank, but unlike normal hierarchies, which are extraordinarily stable in nature, social rank in the sink was very unstable. "At regular intervals during the course of their working hours, these top-ranking males engaged in free-for-alls that culminated in the transfer of dominance from one male to another."

Another social manifestation was what Calhoun called "classes" of rats, which shared territories and exhibited similar behavior. The function of the class, apparently, is to reduce friction between the rats. Normally, there were as many as three classes in a colony.

An increase in population density leads to a proliferation of classes and subclasses. The hyperactive males violated not only the mating mores by invading the burrow when chasing females, but other territorial mores as well. They ran around in a pack, pushing, probing, exploring, testing. Apparently they were afraid only of the dominant male sleeping at the foot of the ramp in the Pen I or IV area, protecting his territory and his harem against all comers.

The advantages to both the species and the individual bestowed by territoriality and stable hierarchical relationships were clearly demonstrated by the rats who occupied Pen I. From the observation window in the top of the room, one could look down and see a large, healthy rat asleep at the foot of a ramp. At the top of the ramp, a small group of hyperactive males might be testing him to see if they could enter. He needed only to open an eye to discourage invasion.

From time to time, one of the females would emerge from a burrow, cross in front of the sleeping male, scamper up the ramp without awakening him, and return later, followed by a pack of hyperactive males who would stop when they reached the top of the ramp. Beyond this point she would not be molested and could bear and rear her young undisturbed by the constant turmoil of the sink. Her measured record of achievement as a mother was ten to twenty-five times that of females in the sink. Not only did she bear twice as many young, but half or better of her young would survive weaning.

Physiological Consequences of the Sink

As with the Sika deer, the sink hit hardest at the female rats and the young. The mortality rate of females in the sink was three and a half times that of the males. Of the 558 young born at the height of the sink, only one-fourth survived to be weaned. Pregnant rats had trouble continuing pregnancy. Not only did the rate of miscarriages increase significantly, but the females started dying from disorders of the uterus, ovaries, and fallopian tubes. Tumors of the mammary glands and sex organs were identified in autopsied rats. The kidneys, livers, and adrenals were also enlarged or diseased and showed signs that are usually associated with extreme stress.

Aggressive Behavior

As Konrad Lorenz, the German ethologist, has made clear in *Man Meets Dog,* normal aggressive behavior has accompanying signals that will extinguish the aggressive impulse when the vanquished has "had enough." Male rats in the sink failed to suppress aggression in each other, and engaged in very extensive, often unprovoked and unpredictable tail biting. This behavior went on for about three months, until the mature rats discovered new ways to suppress tail biting in their fellows. But young rats, who had not learned how to keep their tails from being bitten, were still subject to extensive damage.

The Sink that Didn't Develop

A second series of experiments demonstrated the strategic relationship between the sink and the conditioned need to eat with other rats. In these experiments, Calhoun changed the type of food from pellet to meal, so that food could be eaten quickly. Water, on the other hand, was dispensed from a slow fountain so that rats became conditioned to drinking instead of eating with other rats. This change kept the population more evenly distributed among the pens; because rats normally drink immediately after awakening, they tended to stay in their sleeping area. (For the previous experiment most of the rats had moved to the pen where they ate.) There is some indication that in the second series, a sink would eventually have developed, but for different 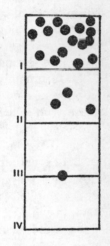 reasons. One male took over Pens III and IV, driving all other rats out. A second male was in the process of establishing territorial rights to Pen II. When the experiment was terminated, *80 per cent of the males were concentrated in Pen I, the remainder, minus one, were in Pen II.*

Summary of Calhoun's Experiments

It is clear from Calhoun's experiments that even the rat, hardy as he is, cannot tolerate disorder and that, like man, he needs some time to be alone. Females on the nest are particularly vulnerable, as are the young who need to be screened from birth to weaning. Also, if pregnant rats are harassed too much, they have increased difficulty in bringing pregnancy to full term.

Probably there is nothing pathological in crowding per se that produces the symptoms that we have seen. Crowding, however, disrupts important social functions and so leads to disorganization and ultimately to population collapse or large-scale die-off.

The sex mores of the rats in the sink were disrupted, and pansexuality and sadism were endemic. Rearing the young became almost totally disorganized. Social behavior of the males deteriorated, so that tail biting broke out. Social hierarchies were unstable, and territorial taboos were disregarded unless backed by force. The extremely high mortality rates of females unbalanced the sex ratio and thus exacerbated the situation of surviving females, who were even more harassed by males during the time they came in heat.

Unfortunately, there is no comparable data on wild rat populations under extreme stress and in the process of collapse with which to compare Calhoun's studies. It is possible, however, that if he had run his studies longer the sink effect would have built up to crises proportions. In fact, Calhoun's evidence certainly points to an imminent crisis. No matter how they are viewed, the rat experiments were both dramatic and complex. Yet it is doubtful that the many interacting factors which combine to maintain a proper population balance could be identified from observations of the white Norway rats alone. Fortunately, however, observation of other species has shed light on the processes by which animals regulate their own density as a function of self-preservation.

THE BIOCHEMISTRY OF CROWDING

How can crowding produce the dramatic results—ranging from aggression through various forms of abnormal behavior to mass die-off—which we have seen in animals as different as the deer, the stickleback, and the rat? Search for answers to this question has produced insights with wide implications.

Two English researchers, A. S. Parkes and H. M. Bruce, who were investigating the differing effects of visual and olfac-

tory stimulation on birds and mammals, reported i
that pregnancy in a mouse is suppressed by the presen
male mouse other than the original mate during the first
days after conception. At first, the second stud males we
allowed to mate with the females during the period of vulnerability. Later it was demonstrated that the mere presence
of a second male in the cage would block pregnancy. Finally,
it was found that blocking would occur if a pregnant female
were introduced into an area from which a male had been
recently removed. Since the male was no longer present to be
seen by the vulnerable female, it was obvious that smell
rather than sight was the active agent. This assumption was
proved when it was demonstrated that destruction of the
olfactory lobe in the brain of the female mouse rendered her
invulnerable to the pregnancy-blocking capacity of the strange
male.

Autopsies of the females whose pregnancies were blocked
showed that the corpus luteum, which holds the fertilized
egg to the wall of the uterus, had failed to develop. Normal
formation of the corpus luteum is stimulated by a hormone,
prolactin, and pregnancy blockage can be prevented by in-
jecting ACTH.

Exocrinology

Through their work Parkes and Bruce have radically modified prevailing theories of the relationship of the body's
delicately balanced chemical control systems to the external
world. The ductless, or endocrine, glands have an influence
on virtually everything the body does and have long been
thought of as a closed system sealed in the body which is
only indirectly linked to the outside world. Parkes' and
Bruce's experiments demonstrated that this is not always the
case. They coined the term "exocrinology" (as contrasted
with endocrinology) to express the expanded view of the
chemical regulators to include the products of odoriferous
glands scattered about the bodies of mammals. Odoriferous
substances are secreted from special glands anatomically situ-
ated in a variety of spots such as between the hoofs of deer,
below the eyes of antelope, on the soles of the feet of mice,

he head of the Arabian camel, and in the
n addition, odoriferous substances are pro-
alia and appear in the urine and feces.

ized that the external secretions of one or-
ly on the body chemistry of other organ-
elp integrate the activities of populations
...ps in a variety of ways. Just as the internal secretions integrate the individual, external secretions aid in integrating the group. The fact that the two systems are interlinked helps to explain in part the self-regulating nature of population controls and the abnormal behavior which follows excessive crowding. One syndrome revolves around bodily responses to stress.

Hans Selye, an Austrian working in Ottawa, whose name has long been associated with studies of stress, demonstrated that animals can die from shock if they are repeatedly stressed. Any increased demand on the organism must be met by the addition of energy. In mammals this source of energy is blood sugar. If repeated demands exhaust the supply of sugar available, the animal goes into shock.

The Sugar-Bank Model

Under the intriguing title "The Hare and the Haruspex," Yale biologist Edward S. Deevey recently explained the biochemistry of stress and shock in an effective metaphor:

> It is possible to speak of vital needs as payable in sugar, for which the liver acts as a bank. Routine withdrawals are smoothly handled by hormones from the pancreas and from the adrenal medulla, which act as paying tellers; but the top-level decisions (such as whether to grow or reproduce) are reserved for the bank's officers, the adrenal cortex and pituitary glands. Stress, in Selye's view, amounts to an administrative flap among the hormones, and shock results when the management overdraws the bank.

> If the banking model is gently dissected, it reveals its first and most important servomechanism: a remarkably bureaucratic hook-up between the adrenal cortex, acting as cashier's office, and the pituitary, as board of directors. Injury and infection are common forms of stress, and in

directing controlled inflammation to combat them the cortex draws cashier's checks on the liver. If the stress persists, a hormone called cortisone sends a worried message to the pituitary. Preoccupied with the big picture, the pituitary delegates a vice-presidential type, ACTH, or adrenocorticotropic hormone, whose role is literally to buck up the adrenal cortex. As students of Parkinson would predict, the cortex, bucked, takes on more personnel, and expands its activities, including that of summoning more ACTH. The viciousness of the impending spiral ought to be obvious, and ordinarily it is; but while withdrawals continue, the amount of sugar in circulation is deceptively constant (the work of another servomechanism) and there is no device, short of autopsy, for taking inventory at the bank.

If the pituitary is conned by persisting stress into throwing more support to ACTH, the big deals begin to suffer retrenchment. A cutback of ovarian hormone, for instance, may allow the cortex to treat a well-started foetus as an inflammation to be healed over. Likewise, the glandular sources of virility and of maternity, though unequally prodigal of sugar, are equally likely to dry up. Leaving hypertension aside (because it involves another commodity, salt, which needn't be gone into just now), the fatal symptom can be hypoglycemia. A tiny extra stress, such as a loud noise . . . corresponds to an unannounced visit by the bank examiner: The adrenal medulla is startled into sending a jolt of adrenalin to the muscles, the blood is drained of sugar, and the brain is suddenly starved. This, incidentally, is why shock looks like hyperinsulinism. An overactive pancreas, like a panicky adrenal, resembles an untrustworthy teller with his hand in the till.

The Adrenals and Stress

The reader will remember that the Sika deer showed greatly enlarged adrenal glands just before and during the die-off. This increase in size was presumably associated with increased demands for ACTH, which were due to increased stress from crowding.

Following this lead, Christian in the late 1950s made a study of seasonal changes in the adrenal glands of wood-

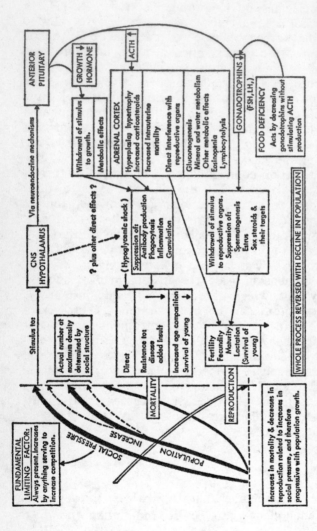

The Biochemistry of Population Control Christian's original (1961) chart showing how endocrine feedback mechanisms lower fertility and decrease resistance to disease in response to population buildup. Note that the process is reversed as population declines. For further explanation see Edward S. Deevey's quote in text under "The Sugar-Bank Model."

chucks. Among the 872 animals collected and autopsied over a four-year period, the mean weight of the adrenals increased as much as 60 per cent from March to the end of June, a period when the male woodchucks were competing for mates, were active for longer portions of the day, and *more of them were concentrated in a given area at the same time.* Adrenal weight declined in July, when the greatest number of animals were active but *aggressiveness* was very low. The weight rose again sharply in August, when there was exten-

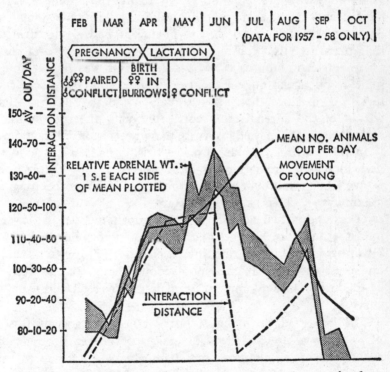

Christian's chart (1963) showing seasonal changes in the weight of woodchuck adrenals in relation to the number of animals. Note how population builds up from March through June accompanied by decreased interaction distance, conflict, stress, and an increase in the weight of the adrenals. Conflicts during the breeding season exacerbate stress. In July, as the young move out, the interaction distance increases and the endocrines return to normal.

sive movement among young woodchucks moving out to establish territories and there were frequent conflicts. Thus, concluded Christian, "it seems that the lack of aggressiveness was the most important consideration initiating the summer decline in adrenal weight."

It is now widely held that the processes of selection which control evolution favor the dominant individuals in any given group. Not only are they under less stress but they also seem to be able to stand more stress. Christian, in a study of the "pathology of overpopulation" showed that the adrenals work harder and become more enlarged in subordinate than in dominant animals. Also, his own studies had demonstrated that there is a relationship between aggressiveness and distance between animals. When aggressiveness was high among male woodchucks during the breeding season, the mean interaction distance between animals increased. The mean weight of the adrenals was correlated with the mean interaction distance, as well as with the number of interactions.

In other words, to paraphrase Christian, when aggressiveness increases, animals need more space. If no more space is available, as occurs when populations are approaching a maximum, a chain reaction is started. A blowup of aggressiveness and sexual activity and accompanying stresses overload the adrenals. The result is a population collapse due to lowering of the fertility rate, increased susceptibility to disease, and mass mortality from hypoglycemic shock. In the course of this process, the dominant animals are favored and usually survive.

The late Paul Errington, a gifted ethologist and professor of zoology at Iowa State University, spent years observing the effects of crowding on marsh muskrats. He came to the conclusion that if collapse were too severe the recovery time was immeasurably prolonged. The English investigator H. Shoemaker showed that the effects of crowding could be very considerably counteracted by providing the right kind of space for certain critical situations. Canaries which he crowded into a single large cage worked out a dominance hierarchy which interfered with nesting of low-ranking birds until they were provided with small cages where pairs could nest and rear their young. The lower-ranking male canaries thus had an inviolate territory of their own and were therefore more successful in producing a brood than they otherwise would have been.

The provision of individual territories for families and the screening of animals from each other at critical times during the mating season can counteract the ill effects of crowding down to and including animals as low on the evolutionary scale as the stickleback.

The Uses of Stress

If we tend to deplore the results of crowding, we should not forget that the stress which it produces has had positive values. Such stress has been an efficient device in the service of evolution, because it employs the forces of *intra*species competition rather than the *inter*species competition which is more familiar to most of us as nature "red in tooth and claw."

There is a very important difference between these two evolutionary pressures. Competition between species sets the stage on which the first types can develop. It involves whole species, rather than different strains of the same animal. Competition within a species, on the other hand, refines the breed and enhances its characteristic features. In other words, intraspecies competition serves to enhance the organism's incipient form.

Present assumptions about the evolution of man illustrate the effects of both pressures. Originally a ground-dwelling animal, man's ancestor was forced by interspecies competition and changes in the environment to desert the ground and take to the trees. Arboreal life calls for keen vision and decreases dependence on smell, which is crucial for terrestrial organisms. Thus man's sense of smell ceased to develop and his powers of sight were greatly enhanced.

One consequence of the loss of olfaction as an important medium of communication was an alteration in the relationship between humans. It may have endowed man with greater capacity to withstand crowding. If humans had noses like rats, they would be forever tied to the full array of emotional shifts occurring in persons around them. Other people's anger would be something we could smell. The identity of anyone visiting a home and the emotional connotations of everything that took place in the home would be matters of public record so long as the smell persisted. The psychotic would begin to drive all of us mad, and the anxious would make us even more anxious. To say the least, life would be much more involved and intense. It would be less under conscious control, because the olfactory centers of the brain are older and more primitive than the visual centers.

The shift from reliance on the nose to reliance on the eye as a result of environmental pressures has completely redefined the human situation. Man's ability to plan has been made possible because the eye takes in a larger sweep; it codes vastly more complex data and thus encourages thinking in the abstract. Smell, on the other hand, while deeply emotional and sensually satisfying, pushes man in just the opposite direction.

Man's evolution has been marked by the development of the "distance receptors"—sight and hearing. Thus he has been able to develop the arts which employ these two senses to the virtual exclusion of all the others. Poetry, painting, music, sculpture, architecture, the dance depend primarily though not exclusively on eyes and ears. So do the communications systems which man has set up. In later chapters, we shall see how the differing emphasis laid on sight, hearing, and smell by cultures which man has developed has led to greatly differing perceptions of space and the relations of individuals in space.

IV

PERCEPTION OF SPACE: DISTANCE
RECEPTORS—EYES, EARS, AND NOSE

. . . we can never be aware of the world as such, but
only of . . . the impingement of physical forces on the
sensory receptors.

F. P. KILPATRICK
Explorations in Transactional Psychology

Study of the ingenious adaptations displayed in the anat-
omy, physiology, and behavior of animals leads to the
familiar conclusion that each has evolved to suit life in
its particular corner of the world . . . each animal also
inhabits a private subjective world that is not accessible
to direct observation. This world is made up of information communicated to the creature from the outside in
the form of messages picked up by its sense organs.

H. W. LISSMAN
"Electric Location by Fishes,"
Scientific American

These two statements pinpoint the importance of the receptors in constructing the many different perceptual worlds
that all organisms inhabit. The statements also emphasize
that the differences in these worlds cannot be ignored. In order
to understand man, one must know something of the nature
of his receptor systems and how the information received
from these receptors is modified by culture. Man's sensory
apparatus falls into two categories, which can be roughly
classified as:

1. The distance receptors—those concerned with examination of distant objects—the eyes, the ears, and the nose.

2. The immediate receptors—those used to examine the
world close up—the world of touch, the sensations we receive
from the skin, membranes, and muscles.

This classification can be broken down even further. The skin, for example, is the chief organ of touch and is also sensitive to heat gain and loss; both radiant and conducted heat are detected by the skin. Hence, strictly speaking, the skin is both an immediate and a distance receptor.

There is a general relationship between the evolutionary age of the receptor system and the amount and quality of information it conveys to the central nervous system. The tactile, or touch, systems are as old as life itself; indeed, the ability to respond to stimuli is one of the basic criteria of life. Sight was the last and most specialized sense to be developed in man. Vision became more important and olfaction less essential when man's ancestors left the ground and took to the trees, as I mentioned in the last chapter. Stereoscopic vision is essential in arboreal life. Without it, jumping from branch to branch becomes very precarious.

VISUAL AND AUDITORY SPACE

The amount of information gathered by the eyes as contrasted with the ears has not been precisely calculated. Such a calculation not only involves a translation process, but scientists have been handicapped by lack of knowledge of what to count. A general notion, however, of the relative complexities of the two systems can be obtained by comparing the size of the nerves connecting the eyes and the ears to the centers of the brain. Since the optic nerve contains roughly eighteen times as many neurons as the cochlear nerve, we assume it transmits at least that much more information. Actually, in normally alert subjects, it is probable that the eyes may be as much as a thousand times as effective as the ears in sweeping up information.

The area that the unaided ear can effectively cover in the course of daily living is quite limited. Up to twenty feet the ear is very efficient. At about one hundred feet, one-way vocal communication is possible, at somewhat slower rate than at conversational distances, while two-way conversation is very considerably altered. Beyond this distance, the auditory cues with which man works begin to break down rapidly.

The unaided eye, on the other hand, sweeps up an extraordinary amount of information within a hundred-yard radius and is still quite efficient for human interaction at a mile.

The impulses that activate the ear and the eye differ in speed as well as in quality. At temperatures of 0°C. (32°F.) at sea level, sound waves travel *1100 feet a second* and can be heard at frequencies of 50 to 15,000 cycles per second. Light rays travel *186,000 miles a second* and are visible at frequencies of 10,000,000,000,000,000 cycles per second.

The type and complexity of the instruments used to extend the eye and the ear indicate the amount of information handled by the two systems. Radio is much simpler to build and was developed long before television. Even today, with our refined techniques for extending man's senses, there is a great difference in the quality of the reproductions of sound and vision. It is possible to produce a level of audio fidelity that exceeds the ability of the ear to detect distortion, whereas the visual image is little more than a moving reminder system that has to be translated before it can be interpreted by the brain.

Not only is there a great difference in the amount and type of information that the two receptor systems can process, but also in the amount of space that can be probed effectively by these two systems. A sound barrier at a distance of a quarter of a mile is hardly detectable. This would not be true of a high wall or screen that shuts out a view. Visual space, therefore, has an entirely different character than auditory space. Visual information tends to be less ambiguous and more focused than auditory information. A major exception is the hearing of a blind person who learns to selectively attend the higher audio frequencies which enable him to locate objects in a room.

Bats, of course, live in a world of focused sound which they produce like radar, enabling them to locate objects as small as a mosquito. Dolphins, too, use very high-frequency sound rather than sight to navigate and locate food. It should be noted that sound travels four times as fast in water as it does in air.

What is not known technically is the effect of incongruity between visual and auditory space. Are sighted people more likely to stumble over chairs in reverberating rooms, for example? Is it easier to listen to someone else if his voice is coming from one readily located spot instead of from several loudspeakers as is characteristic of our P.A. systems? There is some data, however, on auditory space as a factor in performance. A study by J. W. Black, a phonetician, demonstrated that the size and reverberation time of a room affects reading rates. People read more slowly in larger rooms where the reverberation time is slower than they do in smaller rooms. One of my own interview subjects, a gifted English architect, perspicaciously improved the performance of a malfunctioning committee by bringing in line the auditory and visual worlds of the conference chamber. There had been so many complaints about the inadequacy of the chairman that a replacement was about to be requested. The architect had reason to believe that there was more in the environment than in the chairman to explain the difficulties. Without telling his subjects what he was doing, the architect managed to retain the chairman while he corrected environmental faults. The meeting room was next to a busy street whose traffic noises were intensified by reverberations from the hard walls and rugless floors inside. When reduction of the auditory interference made it possible to conduct a meeting without undue strain, complaints about the chairman ceased.

It should be noted here by way of explanation that the capacity of the "public school" upper-class English to direct and modulate the voice is far greater than that of Americans. The annoyance the English experience when acoustic interference makes it difficult to direct the voice is very great indeed. One sees the sensitivity of the English to acoustic space in Sir Basil Spence's successful recreation of the *atmosphere* of the original Coventry cathedral (destroyed during the blitz) while using a new and visually daring design. Sir Basil felt that a cathedral should not only look like a cathedral but should sound like one as well. Choosing the cathedral at Durham as a model, he tested literally hundreds of samples of plaster until he found one that had all the desired acoustic qualities.

Space perception is not only a matter of what can be perceived but what can be screened out. People brought up in different cultures learn as children, without ever knowing that they have done so, to screen out one type of information while paying close attention to another. Once set, these perceptual patterns apparently remain quite stable throughout life. The Japanese, for example, screen visually in a variety of ways but are perfectly content with paper walls as acoustic screens. Spending the night at a Japanese inn while a party is going on next door is a new sensory experience for the Westerner. In contrast, the Germans and the Dutch depend on thick walls and double doors to screen sound, and have difficulty if they must rely on their own powers of concentration to screen out sound. If two rooms are the same size and one screens out sound but the other one doesn't, the sensitive German who is trying to concentrate will feel less crowded in the former because he feels less intruded on.

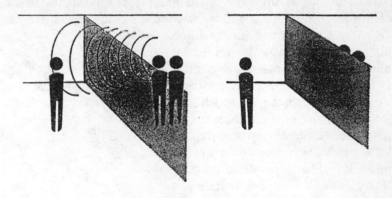

OLFACTORY SPACE

In the use of the olfactory apparatus Americans are culturally underdeveloped. The extensive use of deodorants and the suppression of odor in public places results in a land of olfactory blandness and sameness that would be difficult to duplicate anywhere else in the world. This blandness makes for undifferentiated spaces and deprives us of richness and variety in our life. It also obscures memories, because smell evokes much deeper memories than either vision or sound. Since the American experience of smell is so poorly developed, it seems useful to review briefly the function of olfaction as a biological activity. Here is a sense that must have performed important functions in our past. Hence it is pertinent to ask what roles it did perform and whether some of these are still not relevant, although ignored or even suppressed by our culture.

The Chemical Basis of Olfaction

Odor is one of the earliest and most basic methods of communication. It is primarily chemical in nature and it is referred to as the chemical sense. Serving diverse functions it not only differentiates individuals but makes it possible to identify the emotional state of other organisms. It aids in locating food and helps stragglers to find or follow the herd or the group as well as providing a means of marking territory. Smell betrays the presence of an enemy and may even be used defensively, as in the case of the skunk. The powerful effect of sexual odors is known to anyone who has lived in the country and observed how a bitch in heat will draw dogs for miles around. Other animals have a similarly well-developed olfactory sense. Consider the silk moth, which can locate its mate at a distance of two to three miles, or the cockroach, which also has a phenomenal sense of smell. The equivalent of only thirty molecules of the female sex attractant will excite the male cockroach and make him raise his wings and attempt to copulate. In general, smells are enhanced in dense media, such as sea water, and do not work as well in thin media. Smell is apparently the means that salmon use to return across thousands of miles of ocean to the stream where they were spawned. Olfaction gives way to sight when the medium thins out as it does in the sky. (It would not be effective for a soaring hawk trying to find a mouse a thousand feet below.) Although com-

munication of various types is a major function of smell, it is not popularly conceived of as a signal or message system. And it is only recently that the interrelationship between olfaction (exocrinology) and chemical regulators in the body (endocrinology) has become known.

On the basis of a long history of the study of internal regulators it is known that chemical communication is most suited to the releasing of highly selective responses. Thus chemical messages in the form of hormones work on specific cells programmed to respond in advance while other cells in the immediate vicinity are unaffected. The functioning of the endocrine system in response to stress has been noted in the two preceding chapters. In fact, it would be impossible for advanced organisms to live at all if the highly developed chemical message systems of the body were not working twenty-four hours a day to balance performance with requirements. The body's chemical messages are so complete and specific that they can be said to far exceed in organization and complexity any of the communication systems man has yet created as extensions. This includes language of all forms—spoken, written, or mathematical—as well as the manipulation of various kinds of information by the most advanced computers. The chemical information systems of the body are sufficiently specific and exact to reproduce that body perfectly and keep it operating under a wide range of contingencies.

As we saw in the preceding chapter, Parkes and Bruce demonstrated the fact that, at least under certain circumstances, the endocrine system of one mouse was deeply involved with that of another, and that *olfaction constituted the principal information channel.* There are additional instances, both higher and lower on the evolutionary scale, in which chemical communication constitutes an important, and sometimes the sole, means of integrating behavior. This occurs even on the most elementary levels of life. An amoeba (*Dictyostelium discoideum*), which begins life as a single-celled microscopic organism, maintains a uniform distance from its neighbors by chemical means. As soon as the food supply dwindles, the amoebae, using a chemical locator called acrasin, aggregate into a slug that forms into a stalk ending in a small, round, fruiting body of spores at the top. Discussing "action at a distance" and how these social amoebae are oriented in space, the biologist Bonner, quoted in John Tyler's "How Slime Molds Communicate," *Scientific American*, August 1963, states:

> We were not at the time worrying about what the cells say to one another in the process of marshaling a unified multicellular organism. We had become interested in what might be termed conversations between cell masses and their neighbors. We had raised the level of discourse, in other words, from that of cells to that of organisms composed of numbers of cells. It now appears that the same principle of communication is engaged at both levels.

Bonner and his colleagues demonstrated that the social aggregations of amoebae are evenly spaced. The spacing mechanism is gas, produced by the colony, which blocks overconcentration by maintaining a population density with a ceiling of two hundred fifty cells per cubic millimeter of air space. Bonner was able to increase the density experimentally by placing activated charcoal near colonies of cells. The charcoal absorbed the gas and the population density shot up accordingly, thus demonstrating one of the simplest and most basic of all of the population control systems.

Chemical messages can be of many kinds. Some of them even act across time to warn succeeding individuals when something has happened to a predecessor. Hediger tells how reindeer, approaching a spot where one of their species has recently been frightened, will flee when they smell the scent excreted from the hoof glands of the frightened deer. Hediger also cites experiments by von Frisch, who found that a fluid extract of the crushed skin of a minnow will cause flight reaction in members of the same species. In discussing olfactory messages with a psychoanalyst, a skillful therapist with an unusual record of success, I learned that the therapist could clearly distinguish the smell of anger in patients at a distance of six feet or more. People who work with schizophrenics have long claimed that they have a characteristic odor. Such naturalistic observations led to a series of experiments in which Dr. Kathleen Smith, a St. Louis psychiatrist, demonstrated that rats readily distinguish between the smell of a schizophrenic and a non-schizophrenic. In light of the powerful effect of chemical message systems one wonders if fear, anger, and schizophrenic panic may not act directly on the endocrine systems of nearby persons. One would suspect that this would be the case.

Olfaction in Humans

Americans traveling abroad are apt to comment on the smell of strong colognes used by men living in Mediterranean countries. Because of their heritage of northern European culture, these Americans will find it difficult to be objective about such matters. Entering a taxicab, they are overwhelmed by the inescapable presence of the driver, wholse olfactory aura fills the cab.

Arabs apparently recognize a relationship between disposition and smell. The intermediaries who arrange an Arab marriage usually take great precautions to insure a good match. They may even on occasion ask to smell the girl and will reject her if she "does not smell nice," not so much on esthetic grounds but possibly because of a residual smell of anger or discontent. Bathing the other person in one's breath is a common practice in Arab countries. The American is taught not to breathe on people. He experiences difficulty when he is within olfactory range of another person with whom he is not on close terms, particularly in public settings. He finds the intensity and sensuality overwhelming and has trouble paying attention to what is being said and at the same time coping with his feelings. In brief, he has been placed in a double bind and is pushed in two directions at once. The lack of congruence between U.S. and Arab olfactory systems affects both parties and has repercussions which extend beyond mere discomfort or annoyance. Chapter XII, dealing with the contact of U.S. and Arab culture, will explore these points further. By banishing all but a few odors from our public life, what have Americans done to themselves and what effect does this have on life in our cities?

In the northern European tradition most Americans have cut themselves off from a powerful communication channel: olfaction. Our cities lack both olfactory and visual variety. Anyone who has walked along the streets of almost any European village or town knows what is nearby. During World War II in France I observed that the aroma of French bread freshly removed from the oven at 4:00 A.M. could bring a speeding jeep to a screaming halt. The reader can ask himself what smells we have in the U.S. that can achieve such results. In the typical French town, one may savor the smell of coffee, spices, vegetables, freshly plucked fowl, clean laundry, and the characteristic odor of outdoor cafés. Olfactions of this type can provide a sense of life; the shifts and the transitions not only help to locate one in space but add zest to daily living.

V

PERCEPTION OF SPACE: IMMEDIATE
RECEPTORS—SKIN AND MUSCLES

Much of Frank Lloyd Wright's success as an architect was due to his recognition of the many different ways in which people experience space. The old Imperial Hotel in Tokyo provides the Westerner with a constant visual, kinesthetic, and tactile reminder that he is in a different world. The changing levels, the circular, walled-in, intimate stairs to the upper floors, and the small scale are all new experiences. The long halls are brought to scale by keeping the walls within reach. Wright, an artist in the use of texture, used the roughest of bricks, then separated them by smooth, gilded mortar set in from the surface a full half-inch. Walking down these halls the guest is almost compelled to run his fingers along the grooves. But Wright did not intend that people run their fingers along the grooves. The brick is so rough that to obey this impulse would be to risk mangling a finger. With this device Wright enhances the experience of space by personally involving people with the surfaces of the building.

The early designers of the Japanese garden apparently understood something of the interrelationship between the kinesthetic experience of space and the visual experience. Lacking wide-open spaces, and living close together as they do, the Japanese learned to make the most of small spaces. They were particularly ingenious in stretching visual space by exaggerating kinesthetic involvement. Not only are their gardens designed to be viewed with the eyes, but more than the usual number of muscular sensations are built into the experience of walking through a Japanese garden. The visitor is periodically forced to watch his step as he picks his way along ir-

regularly spaced stepstones set in a pool. At
each rock he must pause and look down to
see where to step next. Even the neck muscles are deliberately brought into play. Looking up, he is arrested for a moment by a
view that is broken as soon as he moves his
foot to take up a new perch. In the use of
interior space, the Japanese keep the edges
of their rooms clear because everything takes
place in the middle. Europeans tend to fill
up the edges by placing furniture near or
against walls. As a consequence, Western

rooms often look less cluttered to the Japanese than they do
to us.

Both the Japanese and the European concept of spatial experience varies from our own, which is much more limited.
In America, the conventional idea of the space needed by
office employees is restricted to the actual space required to
do the job. Anything beyond the minimum requirement is
usually regarded as a "frill." The concept that there may be
additional requirements is resisted, at least in part because of
the American's mistrust of subjective feelings as a source of
data. We can measure with a tape whether or not a man can
reach something, but we must apply an entirely different set
of standards to judge the validity of an individual's feeling of
being cramped.

HIDDEN ZONES IN AMERICAN OFFICES

Because there is so little information on what it is that produces these subjective feelings, I conducted a series of "non-
directed" interviews on people's reactions to office space.
These interviews revealed that the single most important criterion is what people can do in the course of their work
without bumping into something. One of my subjects was a
woman who had occupied a series of offices of different dimensions. Doing the same job in the same organization in a
variety of offices, she noted that these offices provided different spatial experiences. One office would be adequate; another
would not. Reviewing these experiences with her in detail

brought out the fact that, like many people, she had a habit of pushing herself away from her desk and leaning back in her chair to stretch her arms, legs, and spine. I observed that the length of the away-from-desk shove was highly uniform, and that if she touched the wall when she leaned back, the office struck her as too small. If she didn't touch the wall, she considered it ample.

Based on interviews of over one hundred American informants, it would appear that there are three hidden zones in American offices:

1. The immediate work area of the desktop and chair.

2. A series of points within arm's reach outside the area mentioned above.

3. Spaces marked as the limit reached when one pushes away from the desk to achieve a little distance from the work without actually getting up.

An enclosure that permits only movement within the first area is experienced as cramped. An office the size of the second is considered "small." An office with Zone 3 space is considered adequate and in some cases ample.

Kinesthetic space is an important factor in day-to-day living in the buildings that architects and designers create. Consider for a moment American hotels. I find most hotel rooms too small because I can't move around in them without bumping into things. If Americans are asked to compare two identical rooms, the one that permits the greater variety of free movement will usually be experienced as larger. There is certainly great need for improvement in the layout of our interior spaces, so that people are not always bumping into each other. One woman (non-contact) in my sample, a normally cheerful, outgoing person, who had been thrown into a temper for the umpteenth time by her modern but badly designed kitchen, said:

"I hate being touched or bumped, even by people who are close to me. That's why this kitchen makes me so mad when I'm trying to get dinner and someone is always in my way."

Given the fact that there are great individual and cultural differences in spatial needs (see Chapters X through XII), there are still certain generalizations which can be made about what it is that differentiates one space from another. Briefly, what you can do in it determines how you experience a given space. A room that can be traversed in one or two steps gives an entirely different experience from a room requiring fifteen or twenty steps. A room with a ceiling you can touch is quite different from one with a ceiling eleven feet high. In large outdoor spaces, the sense of spaciousness actually experienced depends on whether or not you can walk around. San Marco Square in Venice is exciting not only because of its size and proportions but because every inch of it can be traversed on foot.

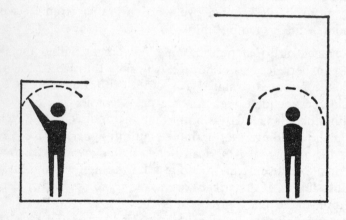

THERMAL SPACE

The information received from the distance receptors (the eyes, ears, and nose) plays such an important part in our daily life that few of us would even think of the skin as a major sense organ. However, without the ability to perceive heat and cold, organisms including man would soon perish. People would freeze in winter and get overheated in summer. Some of the more subtle sensing (and communicating) qualities of the skin are commonly overlooked. These are the qualities which also relate to man's perception of space.

Nerves called the proprioceptors keep man informed of

what is taking place as he works his muscles. Providing the feedback which enables man to move his body smoothly, these nerves occupy a key position in kinesthetic space perception. Another set of nerves, the exterioceptors, located in the skin, convey the sensations of heat, cold, touch, and pain to the central nervous system. One would expect that since two different systems of nerves were employed, kinesthetic space would be qualitatively different from thermal space. This is precisely the case even though the two systems work together and are mutually reinforcing most of the time.

It is only recently that some remarkable thermal characteristics of the skin have been discovered. Apparently, the capacity of the skin both to emit and to detect radiant (infrared) heat is extraordinarily high, and one would assume that this capacity, since it is so highly developed, was important to survival in the past and may still have a function. Man is well equipped both to send and to receive messages as to his emotional state by means of changes in the skin temperature in various parts of the body. Emotional states are also reflected in changes in the blood supply to different parts of the body. Everyone recognizes the blush as a visual sign; but since dark-skinned people also blush, it is apparent that the blush is not just a matter of change in skin coloration. Careful observation of dark-skinned people when they are embarrassed or angry reveals a swelling of the blood vessels in the region of the temples and the forehead. The additional blood, of course, raises the temperature in the flushed area.

New instruments have made possible the study of heat emission, which should eventually lead to research in the thermal details of interpersonal communication, an area previously not accessible to direct observation. The new instruments referred to are infrared detecting devices and cameras (thermographic devices) originally developed for satellites and homing missiles. Thermographic devices are wonderfully adapted to the recording of subvisual phenomena. R. D. Barnes in a recent article in *Science* tells how photographs taken in the dark using the radiant heat of the human body show some remarkable things. Skin color, for example, does not affect the amount of heat emitted; dark skins emit no more and no less heat than light skins. What does have an effect is the blood supply in a given area of the body. These devices confirm the fact that an inflamed area of the body is actually several degrees hotter than the surrounding area, a condition which most of us can detect by touch. Blockages affecting the circulation of the blood and disease (including cancer of the breast in women) can be diagnosed using thermographic techniques.

Increased heat at the surface of someone else's body is detected in three ways: first, by the thermal detectors in the skin, if two subjects are close enough; second, by intensifying olfactory interaction (perfume or face lotion can be smelled at a greater distance when skin temperature rises); and third, by visual examination.

When I was younger, I often observed while dancing that not only were some of my partners hotter or colder than average, but that the temperature of the same girl changed from time to time. It was always at that point, where I found myself establishing a thermal balance and getting interested without really knowing why, that these young ladies would inevitably suggest that it was time to "get some air." Checking on this phenomenon years later, I mentioned thermal changes to several female subjects and learned that they were quite familiar with them. One subject claimed that she could tell the emotional state of her boy friend even at a distance of three to six feet in the dark. She reported that she could detect the point at which either anger or lust was beginning to take over. Another subject used to rely on temperature changes in the chest of her dance partners and would take corrective action before things "went too far."

One might be tempted to scoff at observations such as these if it weren't for a report by one of our scientific investigators of sex. In a paper presented to the American Anthropological Association in 1961, W. M. Masters showed with the use of color slides that a rise in temperature of the skin of the abdomen is one of the very early indications of sexual excitement. Taken by themselves, the reddening of the face in anger, the blush of embarrassment, the red spot between the eyes indicative of the "slow burn," the sweating palms and the "cold sweat" of fear, and the flush of passion are little more than curiosities. Combined with what we know of behavior in lower life forms, they can be seen as significant remnants of displays—behavioral fossils, you might say—which originally served the purpose of letting the other person know what was going on.

This interpretation seems even more plausible when we take into account the possibility suggested by Hinde and Tinbergen that display in birds is probably under the same nervous control as the use of the feathers in cooling and warming. The mechanism apparently functions somewhat as follows: A male bird in the presence of another male gets angry, which sets in motion an elaborate complex of messages (endocrine and nervous) to different parts of the body, preparing the bird for combat. One of the many ensuing changes is an increase in temperature, which in turn results in the puffing out of the feathers as though it were a hot summer day. The mechanism is very similar to the thermostat on the early cars that opened and closed the louvers on the radiator when the motor was hot or cold.

Temperature has a great deal to do with how a person experiences crowding. A chain reaction of sorts is set in motion when there is not enough space to dissipate the heat of a crowd and the heat begins to build up. In order to maintain the same degree of comfort and lack of involvement, a hot crowd requires more room than a cool one. I had occasion to observe this one time when my family and I were traveling to Europe by air. There had been a series of delays, and we were forced to stand in a long queue. Finally we were moved from the air-conditioned terminal to another line outside in summer heat. Even though the passengers were no closer together, the crowding was much more noticeable. The significant factor that changed was the heat. When thermal spheres overlap and people can also smell each other, they are not only much more involved but, if the Bruce effect mentioned in Chapter III has meaning for humans, they may even be under the chemical influence of each other's emotions. Several of my subjects voiced the sentiments of many non-contact peoples (the ones who avoid touching strangers) when they said that they hated to sit in upholstered

chairs immediately after they had been vacated by someone else. On submarines, a frequent complaint of the crew is about "hot bunking," the practice of sharing bunks, so that as soon as one watch "crawls out of the sack" the relieved watch takes their place. We do not know why one's own heat is not objectionable and a stranger's is. Possibly this is due to our great sensitivity to small temperature differences. People seem to respond negatively to a heat pattern that is not familiar.

Interpretation of the awareness (or lack of it) of the many messages that we get from our thermal receptors poses certain problems for the scientist. The process is more complex than is apparent at first. The secretions of the thyroid, for example, alter cold sensitivity; hypothyroidism causes subjects to feel cold, while hyperthyroidism produces the opposite effect. Sex, age, and the individual chemistry are involved. Neurologically, heat regulation lies deep in the brain and is controlled by the hypothalmus. But culture, too, obviously affects attitudes. The fact that humans can exert little or no conscious control over their entire heat system may explain why so little research has been done on the matter. As Freud and his followers observed, our own culture tends to stress that which can be controlled and to deny that which cannot. Body heat is highly personal, and is linked in our minds with intimacy as well as with childhood experiences.

The English language abounds with such expressions as "hot under the collar," "a cold stare," "a heated argument," "he warmed up to me." My experience in conducting proxemic research leads me to believe that these expressions are more than mere figures of speech. Apparently, man's recognition of the changes in body temperature, both in himself and in others, is such a common experience that it has been incorporated into the language.

An additional method of checking on man's response to thermal states in himself and in others is to use one's self as a control. My own increased awareness has taught me that the skin is a much more constant source of information at a distance than I had ever supposed. For example, once when I was attending a dinner party, the guest of honor was holding forth and everyone's attention was focused on him. While listening attentively, I realized that something had caused me to withdraw my hand from the table with reflex speed. I had not been touched, yet an unknown stimulus had produced an involuntary jerk of my hand which startled me. Since the source of the stimulus was unknown, I placed my hand back where it had been before. I then noted the hand of the guest next to me resting on the tablecloth. I remembered vaguely detecting the peripheral visual image of her putting her hand on the table while she listened. My fist had been within heat range, which turned out to be a full two and a half inches! In other instances, I have been fully aware of the heat of people's faces at eleven to eighteen inches as they leaned over me while looking at something in a picture or a book.

The reader can easily test his own sensitivity. The lips and the back of the hand generate a good deal of heat. Placing the back of the hand in front of the face and slowly moving it up and down at different distances enables one to establish a point at which heat is readily detected.

The blind are a good source of data on sensitivity to radiated heat. However, they are unaware of their own sensitivity in the technical sense and do not talk about it until alerted to look for thermal sensations. This was discovered during interviews conducted by a psychiatric colleague (Dr. Warren Brodey) and myself. We were investigating the use of the senses by blind subjects. During the interviews the subjects had mentioned the currents of air around windows and how important windows are to the blind for non-visual navigation, enabling them to locate themselves in a room and also to maintain contact with the outdoors. Hence, we had reason to believe that it was more than a heightened sense of hearing that enabled this group to navigate so successfully. At subsequent sessions with this group, repeated instances were reported in which the radiant heat of objects was not only detected but had been used as an aid in navigation. A brick wall on the north side of a given street was identified as a landmark to the blind because it radiated heat over the total width of the sidewalk.

TACTILE SPACE

Touch and visual spatial experiences are so interwoven that the two cannot be separated. Think for a moment how young children and infants reach, grasp, fondle, and mouth everything, and how many years are required to train children to subordinate the world of touch to the visual world. Commenting on space perception, the artist Braque distinguished between visual and tactile space thus: "tactile" space separates the viewer from objects while "visual" space separates objects from each other. Emphasizing the difference between these two types of space and their relations to the *experience* of space, he said that "scientific" perspective is nothing but an eye-fooling trick—a bad trick—which makes it impossible for the artist to convey the full experience of space.

James Gibson, the psychologist, also relates vision to touch. He states that if we conceive of the two as channels of information in which the subject is actively exploring (scanning) with *both* senses, the flow of sense impressions is reinforced. Gibson distinguishes between active touch (tactile scanning) and passive touch (being touched). He reports that active touch enabled subjects to reproduce abstract objects that were screened from view with 95 per cent accuracy. Only 49 per cent accuracy was possible with passive touch.

Michael Balint, writing in the *International Journal of Psychoanalysis*, describes two different perceptual worlds, one *sight oriented*, the other *touch oriented*. Balint sees the touch oriented as both more immediate and more friendly than the sight oriented world in which *space* is friendly but is filled with dangerous and unpredictable objects (people).

In spite of all that is known about the skin as an information-gathering device, designers and engineers have failed to grasp the deep significance of touch, particularly active touch. They have not understood how important it is to keep the person related to the world in which he lives. Consider Detroit's broad-base behemoths that clog our roads. Their great size, davenport seats, soft springs, and insulation make each ride an act of sensory deprivation. American automobiles are designed to give as little feeling of the road as possible. Much of the joy of riding in sports cars or even a good European sedan is the sense of being in contact with the vehicle as well as with the road. One of the attractions of sailing, in the view of many enthusiasts, is the interplay of visual, kinesthetic, and tactile experiences. A friend who sails tells me that unless he has the tiller in his hand, he has very little feeling of what is happening to the boat. There is no doubt that sailing provides its many devotees with a renewed sense of being in contact with something, a feeling we are denied by our increasingly insulated, automated life.

In times of disaster, the need to avoid physical contact can be crucial. I am not speaking about those incidents of critical overcrowding that induce disaster, like the slave ships with 1.1 to 8.0 square feet per person, but supposedly "normal" situations in subways, elevators, air-raid shelters, hospitals, and prisons. Most of the data used to establish criteria for crowding are inappropriate because they are too extreme. Lacking definitive measures, those who study crowding repeatedly fall back on incidents in which the crowding has been so extreme as to result in insanity or death. As more and more is learned about both men and animals, it becomes clearer that the skin itself is a very unsatisfactory boundary or measuring point for crowding. Like the moving molecules that make up all matter, living things *move* and therefore require more or less fixed amounts of space. Absolute zero, the bottom of the scale, is reached when people are so compressed that movement is no longer possible. Above this point, the containers in which man finds himself either allow him to move about freely or else cause him to jostle, push, and shove. How he responds to this jostling, and hence to the enclosed space, depends on how he feels about being touched by strangers.

Two groups with which I have had some experience—the Japanese and the Arabs—have much higher tolerance for crowding in public spaces and in conveyances than do Americans and northern Europeans. However, Arabs and Japanese are apparently more concerned about their own requirements for the spaces they live in than are Americans. The Japanese, in particular, devote much time and attention to the proper organization of their living space for perception by all their senses.

Texture, about which I have said very little, is appraised and appreciated almost entirely by touch, even when it is visually presented. With few exceptions (to be mentioned later) it is the memory of tactile experiences that enables us to appreciate texture. So far, only a few designers have paid much attention to the importance of texture, and its use in architecture is largely haphazard and informal. In other words, textures on and in buildings are seldom used consciously and with psychological or social awareness.

The Japanese, as the objects they produce indicate so clearly, are much more conscious of the significance of texture. A bowl that is smooth and pleasing to touch communicates not only that the artisan cared about the bowl and the person who was going to use it but about himself as well. The rubbed wood finishes produced by medieval craftsmen also communicated the importance they attached to touch. Touch is the most personally experienced of all sensations. For many people, life's most intimate moments are associated with the changing textures of the skin. The hardened, armorlike resistance to the unwanted touch, or the exciting, ever-changing textures of the skin during love-making, and the velvet quality of satisfaction afterward are messages of one body to another that have universal meanings.

Man's relationship to his environment is a function of his sensory apparatus plus how this apparatus is conditioned to respond. Today, one's unconscious picture of one's self—the life one leads, the minute-to-minute process of existence—is constructed from the bits and pieces of sensory feedback in a largely manufactured environment. A review of the immediate receptors reveals first that Americans who live urban and suburban lives have less and less opportunity for active experiences of either their bodies or the spaces they occupy. Our urban spaces provide little excitement or visual variation and virtually no opportunity to build a kinesthetic repertoire of spatial experiences. It would appear that many people are kinesthetically deprived and even cramped. In addition, the automobile is carrying the process of alienation from both the body and the environment one step further. One has the feeling that the automobile is at war with the city and possibly with mankind itself. Two additional sensory capacities, the great sensitivity of the skin to changes in heat and texture, not only act to notify the individual of emotional changes in others but feed back to him information of a particularly personal nature from his environment.

Man's sense of space is closely related to his sense of self, which is in an intimate transaction with his environment. Man can be viewed as having visual, kinesthetic, tactile, and thermal aspects of his self which may be either inhibited or encouraged to develop by his environment. Chapter VI considers man's visual world and how he builds it.

VI

VISUAL SPACE

Vision was the last of the senses to evolve and is by far the most complex. Much more data are fed to the nervous systems through the eyes and at a much greater rate than through touch or hearing. The information gathered by a blind man outdoors is limited to a circle with a radius of twenty to one hundred feet. With sight, he could see the stars. The talented blind are limited to an average *maximum* speed of two to three miles an hour over familiar territory. With sight, man has to fly faster than sound before he begins to need aids to avoid bumping into things. (At a little over MACH 1, pilots have to know about other planes before they can be seen. If two planes are on a collision course at these speeds, there is no time to get out of the way.)

In man the eyes perform many functions; they enable him to:

1. Identify foods, friends, and the physical state of many materials at a distance.
2. Navigate in every conceivable terrain, avoiding obstacles and danger.
3. Make tools, groom himself and others, assess displays, and gather information as to the emotional state of others.

The eyes are usually considered to be the principal means by which man gathers information. However important their function as "information gatherers," we should not overlook their usefulness in conveying information. For example, a look can punish, encourage, or establish dominance. The size of the pupils can indicate interest or distaste.

VISION AS SYNTHESIS

A keystone in the arch of human understanding is the recognition that man at certain critical points synthesizes experience. Another way of stating this is that man learns while he sees and what he learns influences what he sees. This makes for great adaptability in man and enables him to exploit past experience. If man did not learn as a result of seeing, camouflage, for example, would always be effective and man would be defenseless against well-camouflaged organisms. His capacity to penetrate camouflage demonstrates that he alters perception as a result of learning.

In any discussion of vision it is necessary to distinguish between the retinal image and what man perceives. The talented Cornell psychologist James Gibson, to whom I will repeatedly refer in the course of this chapter, has technically labeled the former the "visual field" and the latter the "visual world." The visual field is made up of constantly shifting light patterns—recorded by the retina—which man uses to construct his visual world. The fact that man differentiates (without knowing that he does so) between the sense impressions that stimulate the retina and what he sees suggests that sensory data from other sources are used to correct the visual field. For a detailed description of the basic distinctions between the visual field and the visual world, the reader is referred to Gibson's basic work, *The Perception of the Visual World*.

As he moves through space, man depends on the messages received from his body to stabilize his visual world. Without such body feedback, a great many people lose contact with reality and hallucinate. The importance of being able to integrate visual and kinesthetic experience has been demonstrated by two psychologists, Held and Heim, when they carried kittens through a maze along the same track on which other kittens were allowed to walk. The kittens that were carried failed to develop "normal visual spatial capacities." They did not learn the mazes nearly as well as the other kittens. Kinesthesia as a corrective to vision was experimentally demonstrated time and again by the late Adelbert Ames and the other transactional psychologists. Subjects viewing a distorted room which looked rectangular were given a stick and told to hit a point near a window. They invariably would miss the mark on the first few tries. As they gradually learned to correct their aim and were able to hit the target with the tip of the stick, they saw the room not as a cube but in its truly distorted shape. A different, more individual example would be the mountain that never looks the same once it has been climbed by the viewer.

Many of the ideas presented here are not new. Two hundred and fifty years ago Bishop Berkeley laid some of the conceptual foundations of modern theories of vision. Even though many of Berkeley's theories were rejected by his contemporaries, they were indeed remarkable, particularly in view of the general state of science at the time. Berkeley argued that man actually judges distance as a consequence of the interrelation of the senses with each other and with past experience. He held that we do not "immediately perceive by sight anything besides light and colors and figures; or by hearing anything but sounds." A parallel is drawn with hearing the sound of an unseen coach. According to Berkeley, one does not, strictly speaking, "hear the coach"; one hears sounds that have become associated in the mind with coaches. Man's ability to "fill in" visual details based on auditory cues is exploited in the theater by the sound effects man. In the same sense, Berkeley denies that distance is immediately seen. Words like "high," "low," "left," and "right" get their primary application from kinesthetic and tactile experience.

. . . Suppose I perceive by sight the faint and obscure idea of something which I doubt whether it be a man, or a tree, or a tower, but judge it to be at the distance of about a mile. It is plain I cannot mean that what I see is a mile off, or that it is an image or likeness of anything which is a mile off, since that every step I take towards it the appearance alters, and from being obscure, small, and faint, grows large, clear and vigorous. And when I come to the mile's end, that which I saw first is quite lost, neither do I find anything in the likeness of it.

Berkeley was describing the highly self-conscious visual field of the scientist and the artist. Those who criticized were basing their judgments on their own culturally patterned "visual worlds." Like Berkeley, only much later, Piaget stressed the relationship of the body to vision and stated that "spatial concepts are internalized action." However, as the psychologist James Gibson has pointed out, there is an interplay between vision and body knowledge (kinesthesia) that was not recognized by Berkeley. There are purely visual cues to the perception of space such as the fact that the visual field expands as you move toward something and contracts as you move away from it. One of Gibson's great contributions lies in making the point explicit.

The need to know more about the basic processes that underlie man's "subjective" experiences has recently been recognized by scientists in widely divergent fields. What has been discovered about the sensory inputs demonstrates that they could not produce the effects that they do in the absence of synthesis at higher levels in the brain. Paradoxically, a door, a house, or a table is always seen as being the same shape and color despite great changes in the angle from which it is perceived. As soon as the eye movement is examined, it is revealed that the image cast on the retina can never be the same because the eye is in constant motion. Once this is recognized it becomes essential to discover the process that enables man to see as stationary that which is recorded on the retina as constantly moving. This feat, accomplished by synthesis within the brain, is duplicated when man listens to people talking.

Linguists tell us that when the details of speech sounds are analyzed and recorded with great consistency and accuracy, it is often difficult to demonstrate clear-cut distinctions between some of the individual sounds. It is a common experience for travelers who land on a foreign shore to discover that they cannot understand a language they learned at home. The people of the country don't sound like their tutor! This can be very disconcerting. Anyone who finds himself in the midst of people speaking a totally unfamiliar language knows that at first he hears an undifferentiated blur of sounds. Only later do the first crude outlines of a pattern begin to emerge. Yet once he has learned the language well, he is synthesizing so successfully that he can interpret an extraordinarily wide range of events. Much that would otherwise have been unintelligible gibberish is now understood.

The theory that talking and understanding is a synthetic process is easier to accept than the idea that vision is synthesized, because we are less aware of actively seeing than we are of talking. No one thinks he has to learn how to "see." Yet if this idea is accepted, many more things are explainable than is possible under the older, more widespread notion that a stable, uniform "reality" is recorded on a passive visual receptor system, so that what is seen is the same for all men and therefore can be used as a universal reference point.

The concept that no two people see exactly the same thing when actively using their eyes in a natural situation is shocking to some people because it implies that not all men relate to the world around them in the same way. Without recognition of these differences, however, the process of translating from one perceptual world to another cannot take place. The distance between the perceptual worlds of two people of the same culture is certainly less than that between two people of different cultures, but it can still present problems. As a young man, I spent several summers with students making archaeological surveys in the high deserts of northern Arizona and southern Utah. Everyone on these expeditions was highly motivated to find stone artifacts, arrowheads in particular. We marched along in single file with the typical head-down, ground-scanning gaze of an archaeological field party. In spite of their high motivation, my students would repeatedly walk right over arrowheads lying on top of the ground. Much to their chagrin, I would lean down to pick up what they had not seen simply because I had learned to "attend" some things and to ignore others. I had been doing it longer and knew what to look for, yet I could not identify the cues that made the image of the arrowhead stand out so clearly.

I may be able to spot arrowheads on the desert but a refrigerator is a jungle in which I am easily lost. My wife, however, will unerringly point out that the cheese or the leftover roast is hiding right in front of my eyes. Hundreds of such experiences convince me that men and women often inhabit quite different visual worlds. These are differences which cannot be attributed to variations in visual acuity. Men and women simply have learned to use their eyes in very different ways.

Significant evidence that people brought up in different cultures live in different perceptual worlds is to be found in their manner of orienting themselves in space, how they get around and move from one place to the next. In Beirut, I once had the experience of having come within a short distance of a building I was looking for. An Arab from whom I asked directions told me where the building was and gestured in the general direction I should go. I could tell by his behavior that he thought he was indicating where the building was, yet I couldn't for the life of me tell which building he was referring to or even which of three streets it was on, all visible from where we were standing. Obviously, we were using two entirely different systems of orientation.

THE SEEING MECHANISM

How there can be such great differences in the visual worlds of two people becomes clearer if it is known that the retina (the light-sensitive part of the eye) is composed of at least three different parts or areas: the fovea, the macula, and the region where peripheral vision occurs. Each area performs different visual functions, enabling man to see in three very different ways. Because the three different types of vision are simultaneous and blend into each other, they are not normally differentiated. The fovea is a small circular pit in the center of the retina containing roughly 25,000 closely packed color-sensitive cones, each with its own nerve fiber. The fovea contains cells at the unbelievable concentration of 160,000 cells per square millimeter (an area the size of the head of a pin). The fovea enables the average person to see most sharply a small circle ranging in size from 1/96 of an inch to 1/4 of an inch (estimates differ) at a distance of twelve inches from the eye. The fovea, also found in birds and the anthropoid apes, is a recent development in evolution. In the apes, its function appears to be associated with two activities, grooming and sharp distance vision required by tree life. In man, needle-threading, removal of splinters, and engraving are some of the many activities made possible by foveal vision. Without it there would be no machine tools, microscopes, or telescopes. In short, no science and no technology!

A simple demonstration illustrates the tiny size of the area covered by the fovea. Pick up any sharp, bright object, such as a needle, and hold it steady at arm's length. At the same time, pick up a similar pointed object in the free hand and slowly move it toward the first object until both points are in a single area of clearest vision and can be seen clearly *without shifting the eyes at all.* The two points have to be virtually overlapping before they can be seen that clearly. The most difficult part is to avoid shifting the eyes away from the stationary point toward the moving point.

Surrounding the fovea is the macula, an oval, yellow body of color-sensitive cells. It covers a visual angle of 3 degrees in the vertical plane and 12 to 15 degrees in the horizontal plane. Macular vision is quite clear, but not as clear and sharp as foveal vision because the cells are not as closely packed as they are in the fovea. Among other things man uses the macula for reading.

The man who detects movement out of the corner of his eye is seeing peripherally. Moving away from the central portion of the retina, the character and quality of vision change radically. The ability to see color diminishes as the color-sensitive cones become more scattered. Fine vision associated with closely packed receptor cells (cones), each with its own neuron, shifts to very coarse vision in which perception of movement is enhanced. Connecting two hundred or more rods to a single neuron has the effect of amplifying the perception of motion while reducing detail. Peripheral vision is expressed in terms of an angle, approximately 90 degrees, on each side of a line extending through the middle of the skull. Both the visual angle and the capacity to detect motion can be demonstrated if the reader will perform the following experiment. Make two fists with the index fingers extended. Move them to a point adjacent to, but slightly behind, the ears. Looking straight ahead, wiggle the fingers and slowly advance both hands until motion is detected. Thus even though man sees less than a one-degree circle sharply, the eyes move so rapidly as they dart around painting in the details of the visual world that one is left with the impression of a much wider clear area than is actually present in the visual field. The fact that attention is focused on foveal and macular vision in co-ordinated shifts also maintains the illusion of broad-band clear vision.

Let us use a limited setting to illustrate the types of information one receives from the different areas of the retina. American convention prohibits staring at others. However, a man with normal vision, sitting in a restaurant twelve to fifteen feet from a table where other people are seated, can see the following out of the corner of his eye. He can tell that the table is occupied and possibly count the people present, particularly if there is some movement. At an angle of 45 degrees he can tell the color of a woman's hair as well as the color of her clothing, though he cannot identify the material. He can tell whether the woman is looking at and and talking to her partner but not whether she has a ring on her finger. He can pick up the gross movements of her escort, but he can't see the watch on his wrist. He can tell the sex of a person, his body build, and his age in very general terms but not whether he knows him or not.

The structure of the eye has many implications for the design of space. These have not to my knowledge been determined or reduced to a set of principles. A few can be suggested, however, with the understanding that design based on knowledge of the structure and function of the eye is only in its infancy. For example, movement is exaggerated at the periphery of the eye. Straight edges and alternate black and white bands are particularly noticeable. This means that the closer the walls of any tunnel or hallway, the more apparent the movement. In the same way, trees or regularly spaced pillars will exaggerate the sense of movement. This feature of the eye causes drivers in countries like France to slow down when they enter a tree-lined road from an open highway. To increase the speed of motorists in tunnels, it is necessary to reduce the number of visual impacts that flash by at eye level. In restaurants, libraries, and public places, cutting down on movement in the peripheral field should reduce the sense of crowding somewhat, whereas maximizing peripheral stimulation should build up a sense of crowding.

STEREOSCOPIC VISION

The reader may have wondered why nothing has been said so far about stereoscopic vision. After all, isn't the sense of visual distance or space due to the fact that man has stereoscopic vision? The answer is yes and no; yes, only under certain very limited conditions. One-eyed people can see in depth very well. Their greatest liability is impaired peripheral vision on their blind side. Anyone who has ever looked in a stereoscope can sense in a minute its limitations and at the same time know the narrowness of any scientific explanation of depth perception based solely on this feature of human vision. Usually, within a few seconds of looking into a stereoscope, there is a strong urge to move the head, to change the view and to see the foreground move while the background stands still. The very fact that the view is stereoscopic emphasizes that it is also fixed and stationary, an illusion.

Gibson, in his book *The Perception of the Visual World*, provides welcome perspective on the conventional view that depth perception is primarily a function of the stereoscopic effect produced by two overlapping visual fields.

It has been commonly believed for many years that the *only* important basis for depth perception in the visual world is the stereoscopic effect of binocular vision. This is a widely accepted opinion in the medical and physiological study of vision, opthalmology. It is the belief of photographers, artists, motion picture researchers, and visual educators who assume that a scene can be presented in true depth only with the aid of stereoscopic techniques, and of writers and authorities on aviation who assume that the only kind of test for depth perception which a flier needs to pass is a test of his stereoscopic acuity. This belief is based on the theory of the intrinsic cues for depth, which is rooted in the assumption that there exists a class of experiences called innate sensations. With the increasing tendency to question this assumption in modern psychology, the belief is left without much foundation. *Depth, we have argued, is not built up out of sensations but is simply one of the dimensions of visual experience.* (Italics mine.)

It is not essential to dwell longer on this point. Putting something in its place will broaden our view somewhat and add to the understanding of the extraordinary processes that man uses in his perception of the visual world. While it is well to recognize that stereoscopic vision is a factor in depth perception at close distance (sixteen feet or less), there are a great many other ways in which man builds an image of the world in depth. Gibson has done much to isolate and identify the elements that go to make up the three-dimensional visual world. His studies date back to World War II when pilots found that in a crisis, having to translate from instrument panel needle readings to a moving three-dimensional world was too time-consuming and could be fatal. Gibson was given the task of developing instruments that would produce an artificial visual world, replicating the real world so that aviators could fly along electronic highways in the sky. Investigating man's various systems of depth perception as he moves through space, Gibson identified not one or two but thirteen! Because the subject is somewhat complex, the reader is referred to the original work, summarized in the Appendix, which should be required reading for all students of architecture and city planning.

It is clear from Gibson's work and from the extensive studies by the transactional psychologists that the visual sense of distance goes far beyond the so-called laws of linear perspective of the Renaissance. An understanding of the many different forms of perspective makes it possible for us to understand what artists have been trying to tell us for the past hundred years. Everything that is known of man's art in all of his various past cultures indicates that there are great differences that transcend mere stylistic convention. In America linear perspective is still the most popular art style for the general public. Chinese and Japanese artists, on the other hand, symbolize depth in quite a different way. Oriental art shifts the viewing point while maintaining the scene as constant. Much of Western art does just the opposite. In fact, a most significant difference between the East and the West although it is reflected in the art far transcends the field of art. Space itself is perceived entirely differently. In the West, man perceives the objects but not the spaces between. In Japan, the spaces are perceived, named, and revered as the *ma*, or intervening interval.

Chapters VII and VIII will examine art and literature as keys to people's perceptual worlds. Only on rare occasions do the worlds of art and science merge. This happened during the Renaissance and again in the late nineteenth and early twentieth centuries when the French Impressionists studied the physics of light. We may now be approaching such a period again. Contrary to popular belief among many experimentally inclined psychologists and sociologists, the productions of artists and writers represent rich, unmined beds of hard data on how man perceives. To be able to distill and identify the essential variables of experience is the essence of the artist's craft.

VII

ART AS A CLUE TO PERCEPTION

The Painter's Eye, a remarkable little book by the American artist Maurice Grosser, affords one of those rare opportunities to learn from the artist himself just how he "sees" his subject and uses his medium to convey this perception.

Of particular interest to the student of proxemics is Grosser's discussion of portraiture. The portrait, he says, is distinguished from any other sort of painting by psychological nearness, which "depends directly on the actual physical interval—the distance in feet and inches between the model and the painter." Grosser sets this distance at four to eight feet. Such a spatial relation of the artist to his subject makes possible the characteristic quality of a portrait, "the peculiar sort of communication, almost a conversation, that the person who looks at the picture is able to hold with the person painted there."

Grosser's ensuing description of how the artist works on a portrait is fascinating not only for what it reveals of technique but also for its lucid discussion of how men perceive distance as a function of social relationships. The spatial relationships he describes are almost identical to those I observed in my research and those Hediger observed in animals.

> At more than thirteen feet away . . . twice the usual height of our bodies, the human figure can be seen in its entirety as a single whole. At this distance . . . we are chiefly aware of its outline and proportions . . . we can look at a man as if he were a shape cut out of cardboard, and see him . . . as something as *having little connection with ourselves.* . . . It is only the solidity and depth we see in nearby objects that produce in us feelings of sympathy and kinship with things we look at. At twice its

height, the figure can be seen at once. It can be comprehended at a glance . . . understood as a unit and a whole. . . . At this distance whatever meaning or feeling the figure may convey is dominated, not by expression or features of the face, but by the position of the members of the body. . . . The painter can look at his model as if he were a tree in a landscape or an apple in a still life—the *sitter's personal warmth does not disturb him.*

But four to eight feet is the portrait distance. At this distance the painter is near enough so that his eyes have no trouble in understanding the sitter's solid forms, yet he is far enough away so that the *foreshortening* of the forms presents him no real problem. Here, *at the normal distance of social intimacy and easy conversation,* the sitter's soul begins to appear. . . . Nearer than three feet, within touching distance, the soul is far too much in evidence for any sort of *disinterested* observation. Three feet is the sculptor's working distance, not the painter's. *The sculptor must stand near enough to his model to be able to judge forms by sense of touch.*

At touching distance, the problems of foreshortening make the business of painting itself too difficult. . . . Moreover, at touching distance, the sitter's personality is too strong. The influence of the model on the painter is too powerful, too disturbing to the artist's necessary detachment, *touching distance* being not the position of visual rendition, but of motor reaction of some physical expression of sentiment, like fisticuffs, or the various acts of love. (Italics mine.)

The interesting point about Grosser's observations is that they are consistent with proxemic data on personal space. Although he does not use the terms, Grosser distinguishes between what I have called intimate, personal, social, and public distances. It is also interesting to note how many specific clues to distance Grosser mentions. They include touching and non-touching, bodily warmth, visual detail and distortion when intimately close, size constancy, stereoscopic roundness, and the increasing flatness that becomes noticeable beyond thirteen feet. The significance of Grosser's observations is not restricted to the distance at which pictures are painted but lies in his statement of the unconscious, culturally molded spatial frames that both the artist and his subject bring to the

PLATE 1 *(above)*. Male walruses sleeping among the rocks on Round Island, Alaska, give a perfect example of contact behavior.

PLATE 2 *(below)*. Non-contact species, such as these swans, avoid touching.

PLATES 3 AND 4. *Personal distance* is the term applied by the animal psychologist H. Hediger to the normal spacing that non-contact animals maintain between themselves and their fellows. The birds sunning on a log and the people waiting for a bus both demonstrate this natural grouping.

PLATES 5 AND 6. These two photographs of people in conversation illustrate two of man's four distance zones. In PLATE 5 the *intimate distance* between the two subjects clearly reflects the aggressive and hostile nature of their feelings at the moment. PLATE 6 shows three acquaintances maintaining the far phase of *personal distance* from each other.

PLATES 7 AND 8. Impersonal business is generally conducted at *social distance*, varying from four to twelve feet depending on the degree of involvement. People who work together tend to maintain close social distance in their standing and seating positions.

PLATE 9. Public distance is well outside the circle of personal involvement. The voice is exaggerated or amplified, and much of the communication shifts to gestures and body stance. This is the distance of public address and theatrical performance.

PLATES 10, 11 AND 12. Visual comprehension of another body changes with distance and, together with the olfactory and tactile sensations experienced, determines to a large extent the degree of involvement with that body.

PLATE 10 (*above*) is a photograph of one eye of the subject taken at intimate distance. The distortion of features and sharp detail provide a visual experience that cannot be confused with any other distance.

In PLATE 11 (*below*) the subject is photographed at personal distance. Visual distortion of the features is no longer apparent while facial details are still discernible. At this distance, the form, substance, and surface textures of objects are prominent and clearly differentiated.

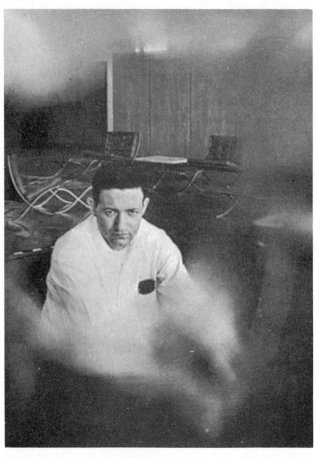

PLATE 12 shows the subject photographed at social distance. The full figure is visible but at the far phase of social distance the finest details of the face, such as the capillaries in the eyes, are lost.

PLATES 13 AND 14. Furniture arrangement in public places has a distinct relationship to the degree of conversation. Some spaces such as railway waiting rooms in which the seating provisions are formally arranged in fixed rows, tend to discourage conversation (sociofugal spaces). Others such as the tables in a European sidewalk cafe, tend to bring people together (sociopetal spaces).

sitting. The artist, trained to be aware of the visual field, makes explicit the patterns governing his behavior. For this reason, *the artist is not only a commentator on the larger values of the culture but on the microcultural events that go to make up the larger values.*

CONTRAST OF CONTEMPORARY CULTURES

The art of other cultures, particularly if it is very different from our own, reveals a great deal about the perceptual worlds of both cultures. In 1959, Edmund Carpenter, an anthropologist working with an artist, Frederick Varley, and a photographer, Robert Flaherty, produced a most remarkable book, *Eskimo*. Much of it is devoted to Aivilik Eskimo art. From plates and text, we learn that the perceptual world of the Eskimo is quite different from our own, and that an important feature of this difference is the Eskimo's use of his senses to orient himself in space. At times in the Arctic there is no horizon separating earth from sky.

The two are the same substance. There is no middle distance, no perspective, no outline, nothing the eye can cling to except thousands of smoky plumes of snow running along the ground before the wind—a land without bottom or edge. When the winds rise and snow fills the air, visibility is reduced to a hundred feet or less.

How can the Eskimo travel across miles of such territory? Carpenter says:

When I travel by car, I can, with relative ease, pass through a complex and chaotic city—Detroit, for example —by simply following a handful of highway markers. I begin with the assumption that the streets are laid out in a grid and the knowledge that certain signs mark my route. Apparently, the Aivilik have similar, though natural, reference points. By and large, *these are not actual objects or points, but relationships;* relationships between, say, contour, type of snow, wind, salt air, ice crack. (Italics mine.)

The direction and the smell of the wind, together with the

feel of ice and snow under his feet, provide the cues that enable an Eskimo to travel a hundred or more miles across
visually undifferentiated waste. The Aivilik have at least
twelve different terms for various winds. They integrate time
and space as one thing and live in acoustic-olfactory space,
rather than visual space. Furthermore, representations of their
visual world are like X rays. Their artists put in everything
they know is there whether they can see it or not. A drawing
or engraving of a man hunting seal on an ice floe will show
not only what is on top of the ice (the hunter and his dogs)
but what is underneath as well (the seal approaching his
breathing hole to fill his lungs with air).

ART AS A HISTORY OF PERCEPTION

For the past few years, Edmund Carpenter, the anthropologist, Marshall McLuhan, Director of Toronto's Center
for Culture and Technology, and I have been studying art
for what it can tell us about how artists use their senses and
how they communicate their perceptions to the viewer. Each
of us has approached the subject in his own way and has
conducted his studies independently of the others. We have,
however, found insights and stimulation in each other's work
and are in agreement that there is much to be learned from
the artist about how man perceives the world. Most painters
know that they are dealing with relative degrees of abstraction;
whatever they do depends on vision and must be translated
into other senses. Paintings can never directly reproduce the
taste or smell of fruit, the touch and texture of yielding flesh,
or the note in an infant's voice that makes the milk begin
to flow in a mother's breasts. Yet both language and painting
symbolize such things; sometimes so effectively that they elicit
responses close to those evoked by the original stimuli. If the
artist is very successful *and the viewer shares the artist's culture,* the viewer can replace what is missing in the painting.
Both the painter and the writer know that the essence of their
craft is to provide the reader, the listener, or the viewer with
properly selected cues that are not only congruent with the
events depicted but consistent with the unspoken language and

culture of their audience. It is the artist's task to remove obstacles that stand between his audience and the events he describes. In so doing, he abstracts from nature those parts
which, if properly organized, can stand for the whole and
constitute a more forceful, uncluttered statement than the
layman might make for himself. In other words, *one of the
principal functions of the artist is to help the layman order
his cultural universe.*

The history of art is almost three times longer than that
of writing, and the relationship between the two types of expression can be seen in the earliest forms of writing, such as
the Egyptian hieroglyphics. However, very few people treat
art as a system of communication which is historically linked
with language. If more people were to take this view they
would find that their approach to art would change. Man is
used to the fact that there are languages which he does not
at first understand and which must be learned, but because
art is primarily visual he expects that he should get the message immediately and is apt to be affronted if he doesn't.

In the next few pages I will try to describe a little of what
it is possible to learn from the study of art and architecture.
Traditionally both art and architecture have been interpreted
and reinterpreted in terms of the contemporary scene. A most
important point to remember is this: modern man is forever
barred from the full experience of the many sensory worlds
of his ancestors. These worlds were inevitably integrated and
deeply rooted in organized contexts which could be fully
understood only by the people of the times. Modern man must
guard against jumping to conclusions too quickly when he
looks at a 15,000-year-old painting on the walls of a cave in
Spain or France. By studying the art of the past it is possible
to learn two things: (a) something from our own responses
about the nature and organization of our own visual systems
and expectations, and (b) some notion of what the perceptual
world of early man *may* have been like. However, our present-
day picture of their world, like the museum pot which has
been patched and mended, will always be incomplete and
only an approximation of the original. *The greatest criticism
one can make of the many attempts to interpret man's past
is that they project onto the visual world of the past the*

structure of the visual world of the present. Projection of this sort is due in part to the fact that few people are aware of what was learned by the transactional psychologists referred to earlier, namely that man actively though unconsciously structures his visual world. Few people realize that vision is not passive but active, in fact, a transaction between man and his environment in which both participate. Therefore, neither the cave paintings of Altamira nor even the temples at Luxor can be counted on to evoke the same images or responses today as when they were created. Temples like Amen-Ra at Karnak are full of columns. To enter them is like walking into a forest of standing petrified logs, an experience which can be quite disturbing to modern man.

The paleolithic cave artist was apparently a shaman who existed in a sense-rich world which he took for granted. Like a very young child, he was apparently only dimly aware that this world could be experienced as separate from himself. He did not understand many natural events, particularly since he had no control over them. Indeed, it is likely that art was one of man's first efforts to control the forces of nature. For the shaman-artist to *reproduce* an image of something may have been his first step in gaining control over it. If this is true, each painting was a separate creative act to bring power and good hunting but was not seen as art with a capital *A.* This would explain why the figures of the deer and the bison of Altamira, while well drawn, are not related to each other, but rather to the topography of the surface of the cave. Later these same magic images were reduced to symbols, which were reproduced again and again, like prayer beads, to multiply the magical effect.

I must explain to the reader that my thinking regarding the interpretation of early art as well as architecture is influenced by two men who devoted their lives to this subject. The first is the late Alexander Dorner, art historian and museum director and student of human perceptions. It was Dorner who taught me the great significance of the work of Adelbert Ames and the transactional school of psychology. Dorner's book, *The Way Beyond Art,* was years and years ahead of its time. I find that I keep returning to it and as my understanding of man grows so does my appreciation for Dorner's insights.

More recently, I have begun to make the acquaintance of the work of the Swiss art historian Sigfried Giedion, author of *The Eternal Present*. While I owe a debt to both these men I must take on my own shoulders full responsibility for re-interpreting their thinking. Both Dorner and Giedion became involved in perceptions. Their work has shown that by study-ing man's artistic productions, it is possible to learn a great deal about the sensory world of the past and how man's per-ception changes as does the nature of his awareness of per-ception. For example, the early Egyptian experience of space was very different from our own. Their preoccupation appar-ently was more with the correct orientation and alignment of their religious and ceremonial structures in the cosmos than with enclosed space per se. The construction and the precise orientation of pyramids and temples on a north-south or east-west axis had magic implications designed to control the su-pernatural by symbolically reproducing it. The Egyptians had a great geometric interest in sight lines and plane surfaces. We also note in Egyptian murals and paintings that everything appears flat and that time is segmented. There is no way of telling whether one scribe in a room is doing twenty different things or twenty different scribes are going about their busi-ness. The classical Greeks developed real sophistication in the complete integration of line and form and in the visual treatment of edges and planes that has seldom been equaled. All of the intervals and straight edges of the Parthenon were carefully executed and arranged so as to appear equal, and deliberately curved so as to look straight. The shafts of the columns are slightly thicker in the middle in order to preserve the appearance of tapering uniformly. Even the foundation is higher in the middle by several inches than at the ends in or-der to make the platform on which the columns rest appear absolutely straight.

People reared in contemporary Western culture are dis-turbed by the absence of inside space in those Greek temples that are sufficiently preserved to give some sense of their original form, such as the 490 B.C. Hephaisteion (also known as the Thesion) in the Agora in Athens. The Western idea of a religious edifice is that it communicate spatially. Chapels are small and intimate while cathedrals are awe inspiring and remind one of the cosmos by virtue of the space they enclose. Giedion states that domes and barrel vaults are present from "the very beginning of architecture . . . and the oldest pointed arch, found in Eridu, goes back to the fourth millennium." However, the potential of the dome and the vault in creating "superspace" was not realized until the first five centuries A.D. by the Romans. The capacity was there but the awareness of the relationship of man to large enclosed spaces was not. Western man did not see himself *in* space until later. As a matter of fact, man has only gradually begun to fully experience himself in space on the level of everyday life using all his senses. As we shall see, evidence for the dissynchronous development of sensory awareness also occurs in art.

For many years I had been puzzled by what seemed to be a paradox in the development of art. Why was it that Greek sculpture was a full thousand years ahead of Greek painting? Mastery of the human figure in sculpture was achieved in classical Greece before the middle of the fifth century B.C. Epitomized in the bronze "Charioteer of Delphi" (470 B.C.), Myron's "Discus Thrower" (460–450 B.C.), and particularly in the "Poseidon" in the Museum at the Acropolis in Athens, there can be no doubt that the ability to express the essence of moving, active, vibrating man in bronze and stone had been recorded forever. The answer to the paradox lies in the fact that sculpture, as Grosser points out, is primarily a tactile and kinesthetic art, and if one views Greek sculpture in these terms it is easier to comprehend. The message is from the muscles and joints of one body to the muscles and joints of another.

I must at this point explain why the reader has not been provided with pictures of the Greek sculpture referred to in the text and why there will be few pictures of paintings later on or why it is that the single chapter in this book where one might expect to find illustrative material contains very little. The decision *not* to illustrate many of the examples was not easy. However, to have done so would have contradicted one of the main points of this book, which is that most communications are in themselves abstractions of events that occur on multiple levels many of which are not at first apparent.

Great art also communicates in depth. Sometimes it takes years or even centuries for the complete message to come through. In fact, one can never be sure that real masterpieces have yielded their last secret and that man knows all there is to know about them. To understand art properly one has to view it many times and enter into a discourse with the artist through his work. To do this there should be no intermediaries, because one needs to be able to perceive *everything*. This rules out reproduction. Even the best reproduction can do no more than remind the viewer of something he has already seen. It is at best a memory aid and should never be confused with or used as a substitute for the real thing. Take the matter of scale, which is an important limiting factor in reproductions. All works of art are created on a certain scale. Altering the size alters everything. In addition sculpture is best experienced when it can be touched and viewed from several angles. Most museums make a great mistake in not letting people touch sculpture. My object in this chapter is to motivate the reader to view and re-view art and to establish his own personal relationships with the world of art.

An analysis of paintings of the Middle Ages reveals how the artist of that time perceived the world. The psychologist Gibson identified and described thirteen varieties of perspectives and visual impressions which accompany the perception of depth. The medieval artist had some knowledge of six of these. *Aerial perspective, continuity of outline,* and *upward location in the visual field* had been mastered. *Texture perspective, size perspective,* and *linear spacing* were partially understood. (See Appendix for a summary of James Gibson's isolates of depth.) A study of medieval art also reveals that Western man had not yet made the distinctions between the visual field (the actual retinal image) and the visual world, which is what is perceived. For man was depicted not as he is recorded on the retina, but as he is perceived (human size). This explains some of the remarkable and peculiar effects in the painting of that time. The National Gallery in Washington has several medieval paintings which illustrate this point: Fra Filippo Lippi's "Rescue of St. Placidus" (mid-fifteenth century) shows the background figures as actually larger than the two monks praying in the foreground, while Sassetta's

"Meeting of St. Anthony and St. Paul" shows the two saints as only slightly larger than two other figures on a path on the side of a hill in the background. Among the thirteenth and fourteenth century paintings in the Uffizi Palace in Florence one can also see numerous examples of the medieval visual world. Gherardo Starnina's "Thebais" depicts a harbor scene viewed from above—the boats in the harbor are *smaller* than the people on the shore behind them, while human scale is held constant at all distances. Much earlier fifth century mosaics at Ravenna are in a different cultural tradition (Byzantine) and are self-consciously and deliberately three-dimensional in *one* effect only. Scrolls and mazes seen at close range illustrate a knowledge that an object, line, plane, or surface that eclipses or overlaps another object or surface will be seen in front of that object (Gibson's continuity of outline). From their mosaics one would gather that the Byzantines were accustomed to living and working at very close range. Even when animals, buildings, or towns are depicted the visual effect is one of extraordinary closeness in Byzantine art.

With the Renaissance three-dimensional space as a function of linear perspective was introduced, reinforcing some medieval spatial concepts and eliminating others. Mastery of this new form of spatial representation began to draw attention to the difference between the visual world and the visual field and therefore the distinction between what man knows to be present and what he sees. Discovery of the so-called laws of perspective where the perspective lines are made to converge on a single point is thought to have been largely the work of Paolo Uccello whose paintings can be seen in the Uffizi Gallery in Florence. Whether Uccello was responsible or not, once the laws of perspective were discovered they spread rapidly and were pushed very quickly to their ultimate expression by Botticelli in an incredible painting called "Calumny." However, there was an inherent contradiction in Renaissance painting. To hold space static and organize the elements of space so as to be viewed from a single point was in reality to treat three-dimensional space in a *two-dimensional manner*. Because the stationary *eye* flattens things out beyond sixteen feet, it is possible to do just this—treat space optically.

The *trompe l'oeil* so popular in the Renaissance and succeeding periods epitomizes visual space as seen from a single point. Renaissance perspective not only related the human figure to space in a mathematically rigid way by dictating its relative size at different distances but caused the artist to accustom himself to both composition and planning.

Since the time of the Renaissance, Western artists have been caught in the mystical web of space and the new ways of seeing things. Gyorgy Kepes, in *The Language of Vision*, mentions that Leonardo da Vinci, Tintoretto, and other painters modified linear perspective and created more space by introducing several vanishing points. In the seventeenth and eighteenth centuries, Renaissance and Baroque empiricism gave way to a more dynamic concept of space which was much more complex and difficult to organize. Renaissance visual space was too simple and stereotyped to hold the artist who wanted to move about and bring new life to his work. New kinds of spatial experiences were being expressed, which led to new awarenesses.

For the past three centuries, paintings have ranged from the highly personal and visually intense statements by Rembrandt to Braque's contained kinesthetic treatment of space. Rembrandt's paintings were not well understood during his lifetime and it would appear that he was the living manifestation of a new and different way of viewing space which today is considered reassuringly familiar. His grasp of the difference between the visual field and the visual world, referred to earlier, was truly remarkable. In contrast to the Renaissance artist, who examined the visual organization of distant objects with the *viewer* held constant, Rembrandt paid particular attention to how one sees if the *eye* is held constant and does not move about but rests on certain specific areas of the painting. For many years I had never really appreciated Rembrandt's knowledge of vision. Increased understanding came unexpectedly one Sunday afternoon in the following way. Visually, Rembrandt's paintings are very interesting and tend to catch the viewer in a number of paradoxes. Details that look sharp and crisp dissolve when the viewer gets too close. It was this effect that I was studying (how close could I get before the detail broke down) when I made an important discovery about

Rembrandt. Experimenting with the viewing of one of his self-portraits, my eye was suddenly caught by the central point of interest in the self-portrait, Rembrandt's eye. The rendition of the eye in relation to the rest of the face was such that the whole head was perceived as three-dimensional and became alive *if viewed at the proper distance*. I perceived in a flash that Rembrandt had distinguished between foveal, macular, and peripheral vision! He had painted a stationary *visual field* instead of the conventional visual world depicted by his contemporaries. This accounts for the fact that looked at from proper distances (which have to be determined experimentally) Rembrandt's paintings appear three-dimensional. The eye must be permitted to center and *rest* on the spot that he painted most clearly and in greatest detail at a distance at which the foveal area of the retina (the area of clearest vision) and the area of greatest detail in the painting match. When this is done, the registry of the visual fields of both the artist and the viewer coincide. It is at this precise moment that Rembrandt's subjects spring to life with realism that is startling. It is also quite evident that Rembrandt did not shift his gaze from eye to eye as many Americans do when they are within four to eight feet of the subject. He painted only one eye clearly at this distance. (See "Oriental Potentate" in the Amsterdam Museum and "Polish Count" in the National Gallery of Art in Washington.) In Rembrandt's paintings one can see a growing awareness and increasing self-consciousness concerning the visual process which quite clearly foreshadows the nineteenth century impressionists.

Hobbema, a Dutch painter contemporary with Rembrandt, communicated the sense of space in a very different, more conventional way for his times. His large, remarkably detailed paintings of country life contain several separate scenes. To be properly appreciated they should be approached within two to three feet. At this distance at eye level, the viewer is forced to turn his head and bend his neck in order to see everything in them. He has to look *up* into the trees and *down* to the brook and *ahead* at the scenes in the middle. The result is truly remarkable. It is like looking out a large plate-glass window on a Dutch landscape of three hundred years ago.

The perceptual world of the impressionists, surrealists, abstract and expressionist artists have shocked succeeding generations of viewers because they do not conform to popular notions of either art or perception. Yet each has become intelligible in time. The late nineteenth and early twentieth century impressionists foreshadowed several features of vision that were later technically described by Gibson and his fellow researchers. Gibson makes a clear-cut distinction between ambient light, which fills the air and is reflected from objects, and radiant light, which is the province of the physicist. The impressionists, realizing the importance of ambient light in vision, sought to capture its quality as it filled the air and was reflected from objects. Monet's paintings of the Cathedral at Rouen, all depicting the same façade but under different conditions of light, are as explicit an illustration of the role of ambient light in vision as one could expect to find. The important point about the impressionists is that they shifted their emphasis from the viewer back out into space again. They were self-consciously trying to understand and depict what happened in space. Sisley, who died in 1899, was like most impressionists a master of aerial perspective. Degas, Cezanne, and Matisse all recognized the built-in, containing and delineating quality of lines symbolizing edges. Recent research on the visual cortex of the brain shows that the brain "sees" most clearly in terms of edges. Edges like Mondrian's apparently produce a sort of cortical jolt beyond that experienced in nature. Raoul Dufy caught the importance of the after-image in the transparently luminous quality of his paintings. Braque showed clearly the relationship between the visual and the kinesthetic senses by consciously striving to convey the *space of touch*. The essence of Braque is almost impossible to get from reproductions. There are many reasons for this but one of them is that the surfaces of Braque's paintings are highly textured. It is the texture that pulls you in close so that you are in reach of the objects he has painted. Properly hung and viewed at the correct distance, Braque's paintings are incredibly realistic. Yet it is impossible to know this from a reproduction. Utrillo is a captive of visual space perspective, though freer than the Renaissance artists. He does not try to remake nature; yet he somehow manages to convey the impression that you can walk around in his spaces. Paul Klee relates time to space and the dynamic perception of changing space as one moves through it. Chagall, Miró, and Kandinsky all seem to know that pure colors—especially red, blue, and green—come to a focus at different points in reference to the retina and that extreme depth can be achieved with color alone.

In recent years, the sense-rich work of Eskimo artists has been cherished by collectors of modern art, partly because the Eskimo approach is similar in many ways to that of Klee, Picasso, Braque, and Moore. The difference is this: everything the Eskimo does is influenced by his marginal existence and is related to highly specialized adaptations to a hostile, demanding environment which allows almost no margin for error. The modern artists of the West, on the other hand, have through their art begun to consciously mobilize the senses and to eliminate some of the translation processes required by objective art. The art of the Eskimo tells us that he lives in a sense-rich environment. The work of modern artists tells us just the opposite. Perhaps this is the reason why so many people find contemporary art quite disturbing.

One cannot in a few pages do justice to the history of man's growing awareness; first of himself, second of his environment, then of himself scaled to his environment, and finally of the transaction between himself and his environment. It is only possible to sketch in the broad outlines of this story, which demonstrates more and more clearly that man has inhabited many different perceptual worlds and that art constitutes one of the many rich sources of data on human perception. The artist himself, his work, and the study of art in a cross-cultural context all provide valuable information not just of content but even more important of the *structure* of man's different perceptual worlds. Chapter VIII explores the relationship of content and structure and draws examples from another art form, literature, that is also rich in data.

VIII

THE LANGUAGE OF SPACE

Franz Boas was the first anthropologist to emphasize the relationship between language and culture. He did this in the most simple and obvious way, by analyzing the lexicon of two languages, revealing the distinctions made by people of different cultures. For example, to most Americans who are not ski buffs snow is just part of the weather and our vocabulary is limited to two terms, snow and slush. In Eskimo, there are many terms. Each describes snow in a different state or condition, clearly revealing a dependence on an accurate vocabulary to describe not just weather but a major environmental feature. Since Boas' time anthropologists have learned more and more about this most important relationship—language to culture—and they have come to use language data with great sophistication.

Lexical analyses are usually associated with studies of the so-called exotic cultures of the world. Benjamin Lee Whorf, in *Language, Thought, and Reality,* went further than Boas. He suggested that every language plays a prominent part in actually molding the perceptual world of the people who use it.

We dissect nature along lines laid down by our native languages. The categories and types that we isolate from the world of phenomena we do not find there . . . on the contrary, the world is presented in a kaleidoscopic flux of impressions which has to be organized by our minds—and this means largely by the linguistic systems in our minds. We cut nature up, organize it into concepts, and ascribe significances as we do, largely because we are parties to an agreement to organize it in this way—an agreement that holds throughout our speech community and is codified in the patterns of our language. The agreement is, of course, an implicit and unstated one, *but its terms are absolutely obligatory;* we cannot talk at all except by subscribing to the organization and classification of data which the agreement decrees.

Continuing, Whorf notes points which are significant for modern science.

> . . . *no individual is free to describe nature with absolute impartiality but is constrained to certain modes of interpretation even while he thinks himself most free.* (Italics mine.)

Whorf spent years in the study of Hopi, the language of Indians who live on the northern Arizona desert mesas. Few, if any, white men can claim to have mastered the Hopi language on the highest levels of fluency, though some do better than others. Whorf discovered part of the difficulty when he began to understand the Hopi concepts of time and space. In Hopi, there is no word which is equivalent to "time" in English. Because both time and space are inextricably bound up in each other, elimination of the time dimension alters the spatial one as well. "The Hopi thought world," says Whorf, "has no imaginary space . . . it may not locate thought dealing with real space anywhere but in real space, nor insulate space from the effects of thought." In other words, the Hopi cannot, as we think of it, "imagine" a place such as the missionary's heaven or hell. Apparently, to them there is no abstract space, something which gets filled with objects. Even the spatial imagery of English is foreign to them. To speak of "grasping" a certain "line" of reasoning, or "getting the point" of an argument, is nonsense to the Hopi.

Whorf also compared English and Hopi vocabularies. Even though the Hopi build substantial stone houses, they have a dearth of words for three-dimensional spaces; few equivalents of room, chamber, hall, passage, crypt, cellar, attic, and the like. Furthermore, he noted, "Hopi society does not reveal any individual proprietorship or relationship of rooms." The Hopi concept of a room is apparently somewhat like a small universe because "hollow spaces like room, chamber, hall are not really *named* as objects are, but are rather located; i.e., positions of other things are specified so as to show their location in such hollow space."

Antoine de St.-Exupéry wrote and thought in French. Like other writers, he was preoccupied with both language and space and expressed his thoughts concerning the externalizing integrating functions of language in *Flight to Arras.*

> What is distance? I know that nothing which truly concerns man is calculable, weighable, measurable. True distance is not the concern of the eye; it is granted only to the spirit. Its value is the value of language, for it is language which binds things together.

Edward Sapir, who was Whorf's teacher and mentor, also speaks with suggestive force about the relation of man to the so-called objective world.

> It is quite an illusion to imagine that one adjusts to reality essentially without the use of language and that language is merely an incidental means of solving specific problems of communication or reflection. The fact of the matter is that the "real world" is to a large extent built up on the language habit of the group.

Sapir's and Whorf's influence has extended far beyond the narrow confines of descriptive linguistics and anthropology. It was their thinking that caused me to consult the pocket Oxford dictionary and extract from it all terms referring to space or having spatial connotations, such as: together, distant, over, under, away from, linked, enclosed, room, wander, fell, level, upright, adjacent, congruent, and so on. A preliminary listing uncovered close to five thousand terms that could be classified as referring to space. This is *20 per cent* of the words listed in the pocket Oxford dictionary. Even deep familiarity with my own culture had not prepared me for this discovery.

Using the historical approach, the modern French writer Georges Matoré, in *L'Espace Humain,* analyzes metaphors in literary texts as a means of arriving at a concept of what he calls the unconscious geometry of human space. His analysis indicates a great shift from the spatial imagery of the Renaissance, which was geometric and intellectual, to an emphasis on the "sensation" of space. Today, the idea of space employs more *movement* and goes beyond the visual to a much deeper sensual space.

LITERATURE AS A KEY TO PERCEPTION

Matoré's analysis of literature is similar in some respect to one I employed in the course of my research. Writers, like painters, are often concerned with space. Their success in communicating perception depends upon the use of visual and other clues to convey *different* degrees of closeness. In light of all that had been done with language, it seemed possible, therefore, that a study of literature might produce data on space perception against which I could check information obtained from other sources. The question I asked myself was whether one could use literary texts as data rather than simply as descriptions. What would be the result if, instead of regarding the author's images as literary conventions, we were to examine them very closely as highly patterned reminder systems which released memories? To do this, it was necessary to study literature, not merely for enjoyment or to grasp the overall theme or plot, but self-consciously in order to identify the crucial components of the message that the author provided the reader to build up his own sensations of space. It must be remembered that communications are on many levels; what is relevant on one level may not be on another. My procedure was to strip out the level that contained references to the sensory data described in Chapters IV, V, and VI. The passages that follow are of necessity taken out of context and therefore lose some of their original meaning. Even so, they reveal how great writers perceive and communicate the meaning and uses of distance as a significant cultural factor in interpersonal relations.

According to Marshall McLuhan, the first use of three-dimensional visual perspective in literature occurred in *King Lear*. Edgar seeks to persuade the blinded Gloucester that they stand atop the cliffs at Dover.

Come on, sir; here's the place: stand still. How fearful
And dizzy 'tis to cast one's eyes so low!
The crows and choughs that wing the midway air
Show scarce so gross as beetles: half way down
Hangs one that gathers samphire, dread trade!
Methinks he seems no bigger than his head:
The fishermen that walk upon the beach
Appear like mice; and yond tall anchoring bark
Diminish'd to her cock; her cock, a buoy
Almost too small for sight: The murmuring surge,
That on the unnumber'd idle pebbles chafes
Cannot be heard so high. I'll look no more,
Lest my brain turn and the deficient sight
Topple down headlong.

Image is piled on visual image to reinforce the effect of
distance seen from a height. The passage comes to a climax
with the use of sound or lack of it. At the end, as at the beginning, the sense of dizziness is evoked. The reader almost
feels himself sway with Gloucester.

Thoreau's *Walden* was published over a century ago, but
it might have been written yesterday.

One inconvenience I sometimes experienced in so small
a house, was the difficulty of getting to a sufficient distance from my guest when we began to utter the big
thoughts in big words. You want room for your thoughts
to get into sailing trim and run a course or two before
they make their port. The bullet of your thought must
have overcome its lateral and ricochet motion and fallen
into its last and steady course before it reaches the ear of
the hearer, else it may plough out again through the side
of his head. Also our sentences wanted room to unfold
and form their columns in the interval. Individuals, like
nations, must have suitable broad and natural boundaries,
even a considerable neutral ground, between them. . . .
In my house we were so near that we could not begin
to hear. . . . If we are merely loquacious and loud talk-
ers, then we can afford to stand very near together, cheek
by jowl, and feel each other's breath; but if we speak
reservedly and thoughtfully we want to be farther apart,
that all animal heat and moisture may have a chance to
evaporate.

In this one short passage, Thoreau says much that applies to points made elsewhere in this volume. His sensitivity to the need to stay outside the olfactory and thermal zones (the zones within which one can smell breath and feel the heat from another's body), and his pushing against the wall to get more space in which to voice the big thought, point up some of the unconscious distance-sensing and distance-setting mechanisms.

I first read Butler's novel *The Way of All Flesh* as a boy. His vivid spatial images have remained with me ever since. Any writing that stays with a reader for thirty-five years is worth another look, so I reread Butler. The scene is played on a sofa which Christina, Ernest's mother, uses to psychological advantage when sweating confessions out of her son. Christina is speaking to Ernest:

> "My dearest boy," began his mother *taking hold of his hand* and placing it within her own, "promise me never to be afraid either of your dear papa or of me; promise me this, my dear, as you love me, promise it to me," and *she kissed* him again and again *and stroked his hair*. But with her other hand she still kept hold of his; she had got him and she meant to keep him. . . .
>
> "Of your *inner* life, my dear, we know nothing beyond such scraps as we can glean in spite of you, from little things which escape you almost before you know that you have said them."
>
> The boy winced at this. It made him feel *hot and uncomfortable* all over. He knew well how careful he ought to be, and yet, do what he could, from time to time his forgetfulness of the part betrayed him into unreserve. His mother *saw that he winced*, and enjoyed the scratch she had given him. Had she felt less confident of victory, she had better have foregone the pleasure of touching as it were the eyes at the end of the snail's horns in order to enjoy seeing the snail draw them in again—but she knew that when she had got him well down into the sofa, and held his hand, she had the enemy almost absolutely at her mercy, and could do pretty much what she liked. . . . (Italics mine.)

Butler's use of intimate distance is intense and accurate. The effect of physical closeness and contact, the tone of voice, the hot flush of anxiety, the perception of his wince show how effectively and purposefully Ernest's personal "bubble" had been penetrated.

One of Mark Twain's trademarks was the distortion of space. The reader sees and hears things that are impossible at distances that are impossible. Living on the edge of the Great Plains, Mark Twain was under the expansive influence of the frontier. His images push, pull, stretch, and squeeze until the reader feels giddy. His incredible sense of the spatial paradox is illustrated in *Captain Stormfield's Visit to Heaven*. Captain Stormfield has been on his journey to heaven for thirty years and is describing to his friend Peters a race he had with an uncommonly large comet.

> By and by I closed up abreast of his tail. Do you know what it was like? It was like a gnat closing up on the continent of America. I forged along. By and by I had sailed along his coast for a little upwards of a hundred and fifty million miles, and then I could see by the shape of him that I hadn't even got up to his waistband yet.

Then follows a description of the race, the excitement and interest among the "hundred billion passengers" who "swarmed up from below."

> Well, sir, I gained and gained, little by little, till at last I went skimming sweetly by the magnificent old conflagration's nose. By this time the captain of the comet had been rousted out, and he stood there in the red glare for'ard, by the mate, in his shirtsleeves and slippers, his hair all rats' nests and one suspender hanging, and how sick those two men did look! I just simply couldn't help putting my thumb to my nose as I glided away and singing out:
> "Ta-ta! ta-ta! Any word to send to your family?"
> Peters, it was a mistake. Yes, sir, I've often regretted that—it was a mistake.

Stripped of the paradoxical there are a number of very real distances and details that can be observed in Mark Twain's account. This is because all descriptions, if they are valid, must maintain a consistency between the details perceived and the distances at which these details can actually be discerned; the state of disarray of the captain's hair, and the expressions on the mate's and captain's faces. These observations are only possible within the closest range of public distance (Chapter X). Then there is the distance that Stormfield is from Peters, which is quite close.

St.-Exupéry had an exquisite sense of personal and intimate space as well as knowledge of how to use the body and the senses to communicate. In the following passages from *Night Flight* three short sentences describe three senses and as many distances.

> Rising, she opened the window and felt the wind on her face. Their room overlooked Buenos Aires. A dance was going on in a house near by and the music came to her upon the wind, for this was the hour of leisure and amusement.

A little later while her husband the aviator still sleeps.

> . . . She looked at the strong arms which, in an hour, would decide the fortune of the Europe mail, bearing a high responsibility, like a city's fate.
> . . . Wild things they were, those hands of his, and only tamed to tenderness; their real task was dark to her. She knew this man's smile, his gentle ways of love, but not his godlike fury in the storm. She might snare him in a fragile net of music, love and flowers, but, at each departure, he would break forth without, it seemed to her, the least regret. He opened his eyes, "What time is it?" "Midnight."

In *The Trial,* Kafka contrasts northern and southern European behavior. His conventions regarding olfactory distance are revealed in the following passage:

> He answered with a few polite formalities which the Italian received with another laugh, meanwhile nervously stroking his bushy iron-grey mustache. This mustache was obviously perfumed; one was almost tempted to go close up and have a sniff at it.

Kafka was very conscious of his *body* and its *space requirements for movement.* His criterion for crowding was set in terms of restrictions on movement.

After taking leave of the Manager he pressed up to K. so close that K. had to push his chair back in order to have any freedom of movement.

. . . K. caught sight of a small side pulpit attached to a pillar almost immediately adjoining the choir. . . . It was so small that from the distance it looked like an empty niche intended for a statue. There was certainly no room for the preacher *to take a full step backwards* from the balustrade. The vaulting of the stone canopy, too, began very low down and curved forward, . . . in such a way that a medium-sized man could not stand upright beneath it but would have to keep leaning over the balustrade. The whole structure was designed to harass the preacher; . . ." (Italics mine.)

Kafka's use of the word "harass" shows awareness of the communicative significance of architecture. His oppressive kinesthetic spaces release in the reader hidden feelings engendered by past architectural harassments, reminding him again that his body is something more than a shell, a passive occupant of *x* number of cubic feet.

From the Japanese novelist Yasunari Kawabata one gets some of the flavor of Japanese sense modalities. The first scene quoted below is out in the open. The second is more intimate. Shifting sensory involvements and their associated moods characterize this novel.

He had to go to the post office before it closed, he said, and the two of them left the room.

But at the door of the inn he was seduced by the mountain, strong with the smell of new leaves. He started climbing roughly up to it.

When he was pleasantly tired, he turned sharply around and tucking the skirts of his kimono into his obi, he ran headlong back down the slope.

Back in the inn Shimamura, about to return to Tokyo, is talking to his geisha:

. . . as she smiled, she thought of "then" and Shimamura's words gradually colored her whole body. When she bowed her head, . . . he could see that even her back under her kimono was flushed a deep red. Set off by the color of her hair, the moist sensuous skin was as if laid naked before him.

If one examines literature for structure rather than content, it is possible to find things that will shed light on historical trends and shifts in sense modalities. There is no doubt in my mind but that such shifts are highly relevant to the type of environment that man finds most congenial at different times and for different cultures. Whether I have, with this brief review, made my point—that literature is, in addition to everything else, a source of data on man's use of his senses—remains to be seen. To me at least the historical and cultural differences are quite obvious. These differences may not, however, be equally clear to those who read for content alone.

The next two chapters deal with the same data but from a different point of view; how man structures space as fixed, semifixed, or moving, as well as the several distances he uses in interacting with his fellows. In other words, it describes the building blocks that should be used in designing our homes and our cities.

IX

THE ANTHROPOLOGY OF SPACE:
AN ORGANIZING MODEL

Territoriality, spacing, and population control were discussed earlier in this book. *Infraculture* is the term I have applied to behavior on lower organizational levels that underlie culture. It is part of the proxemic classification system and implies a specific set of levels of relationships with other parts of the system. As the reader will remember, the term proxemics is used to define the interrelated observations and theories of man's use of space.

Chapters IV, V, and VI were devoted to the senses, the physiological base shared by all human beings, to which culture gives structure and meaning. It is this *pre*cultural sensory base to which the scientist must inevitably refer in comparing the proxemic patterns of Culture A with those of Culture B. Thus, we have already considered two proxemic manifestations. One, the *infra*cultural, is behavioral and is rooted in man's biological past. The second, *pre*cultural, is physiological and very much in the present. The third, the *micro*cultural level, is the one on which most proxemic observations are made. Proxemics as a manifestation of microculture has three aspects: fixed-feature, semifixed-feature, and informal.

Although proper translation from level to level is ordinarily quite complex, it should be attempted by the scientist from time to time if only for the sake of perspective. Without comprehensive systems of thought which tie levels together, man develops a kind of schizoid detachment and isolation that can be very dangerous. If, for example, civilized man continues to ignore the data obtained on the infracultural level about the consequences of crowding, he runs the risk of developing the equivalent of the behavioral sink, if indeed he has not already done so. The experience of James Island deer chillingly recalls the Black Death which killed off two-thirds of Europe's population in the mid-fourteenth century. Though this great human die-off was due directly to *Bacillis pestis,* the effect was undoubtedly exacerbated by lowered resistance from the stressfully crowded life in medieval towns and cities.

The methodological difficulty in translating from level to level stems from the *essential indeterminacy of culture,* which I discussed in *The Silent Language.* Cultural indeterminacy is a function of the many different levels on which cultural events occur and the fact that it is virtually impossible for an observer to examine simultaneously with equal degrees of precision something occurring on two or more widely separated analytic or behavioral levels. The reader can test this for himself by simply concentrating on the phonetic details of speech (the way sounds actually are made) and at the same time trying to talk eloquently. I do not mean simply to enunciate clearly but to think about where you place your tongue, how you hold your lips, whether your vocal chords are vibrating or not, and how you are breathing with each syllable. The indeterminancy referred to here requires additional comment. All organisms are highly dependent on redundancy; that is, information received from one system is backed up by other systems in case of failure. Man himself is also programmed by culture in a massively redundant way. If he weren't, he could not talk or interact at all; it would take too long. Whenever people talk, they supply only part of the message. The rest is filled in by the listener. Much of what is *not* said is taken for granted. However, cultures vary in what is left unsaid. To an American, it is superfluous to have to indicate to a shoeshine boy the color of the paste to be used. But in Japan, Americans who do not indicate this may send out brown shoes only to have them returned black! The function of the conceptual model and the classification system, therefore, is to make explicit the taken-for-granted parts of communications and to indicate relationships of the parts to each other.

What I learned from my research on the infracultural level was also very helpful in the creation of models for work on the cultural level of proxemics. Contrary to popular belief,

territorial behavior for any given stage of life (such as courting or rearing the young) is quite fixed and rigid. The
boundaries of the territories remain reasonably constant, as
do the locations for specific activities within the territory,
such as sleeping, eating, and nesting. The territory is in every
sense of the word an extension of the organism, which is
marked by visual, vocal, and olfactory signs. Man has created
material extensions of territoriality as well as visible and invisible territorial markers. Therefore, because territoriality is
relatively fixed, I have termed this type of space on the
proxemic level *fixed-feature space*. The next section will be
devoted to fixed-feature space, followed by discussions of
semifixed-feature and informal space.

FIXED-FEATURE SPACE

Fixed-feature space is one of the basic ways of organizing
the activities of individuals and groups. It includes material
manifestations as well as the hidden, internalized designs that
govern behavior as man moves about on this earth. Buildings
are one expression of fixed-feature patterns, but buildings are
also grouped together in characteristic ways as well as being
divided internally according to culturally determined designs.
The layout of villages, towns, cities, and the intervening
countryside is not haphazard but follows a plan which changes
with time and culture.

Even the inside of the Western house is organized spatially.
Not only are there special rooms for special functions—food
preparation, eating, entertaining and socializing, rest, recu-
peration, and procreation—but for sanitation as well. *If*, as
sometimes happens, either the artifacts or the activities associated with one space are transferred to another space, this
fact is immediately apparent. People who "live in a mess" or
a "constant state of confusion" are those who fail to classify
activities and artifacts according to a uniform, consistent, or
predictable spatial plan. At the opposite end of the scale is
the assembly line, a precise organization of objects in *time*
and *space*.

Actually the present internal layout of the house, which

Americans and Europeans take for granted, is quite recent. As Philippe Ariès points out in *Centuries of Childhood*, rooms had no fixed functions in European houses until the eighteenth century. Members of the family had no privacy as we know it today. There were no spaces that were sacred or specialized. Strangers came and went at will, while beds and tables were set up and taken down according to the moods and appetites of the occupants. Children dressed and were treated as small adults. It is no wonder that the concept of childhood and its associated concept, the nuclear family, had to await the specialization of rooms according to function and the separation of rooms from each other. In the eighteenth century, the house altered its form. In French, *chambre* was distinguished from *salle*. In English, the function of a room was indicated by its name—bedroom, living room, dining room. Rooms were arranged to open into a corridor or hall, like houses into a street. No longer did the occupants pass through one room into another. Relieved of the Grand Central Station atmosphere and protected by new spaces, the family pattern began to stabilize and was expressed further in the form of the house.

Goffman's *Presentation of Self in Everyday Life* is a detailed, sensitive record of observations on the relationship of the façade that people present to the world and the self they hide behind it. The use of the term façade is in itself revealing. It signifies recognition of levels to be penetrated and hints at the functions performed by architectural features which provide screens behind which to retire from time to time. The strain of keeping up a façade can be great. Architecture can and does take over this burden for people. It can also provide a refuge where the individual can "let his hair down" and be himself.

The fact that so few businessmen have offices in their homes cannot be solely explained on the basis of convention and top management's uneasiness when executives are not visibly present. I have observed that many men have two or more distinct personalities, one for business and one for the home. The separation of office and home in these instances helps to keep the two often incompatible personalities from conflicting and may even serve to stabilize an idealized version of each which conforms to the projected image of both architecture and setting.

The relationship of fixed-feature space to personality as well as to culture is nowhere more apparent than in the kitchen. When micropatterns interfere as they do in the kitchen, it is more than just annoying to the women I interviewed. My wife, who has struggled for years with kitchens of all types, comments on male design in this way: "If any of the men who designed this kitchen had ever worked in it, they wouldn't have done it this way." The lack of congruence between the design elements, female stature and body build (women are not usually tall enough to reach things), and the activities to be performed, while not obvious at first, is often beyond belief. The size, the shape, the arrangement, and the placing in the house all communicate to the women of the house how much or how little the architect and designer knew about fixed-feature details.

Man's feeling about being properly oriented in space runs deep. Such knowledge is ultimately linked to survival and sanity. To be disoriented in space is to be psychotic. The difference between acting with reflex speed and having to stop to think in an emergency may mean the difference between life and death—a rule which applies equally to the driver negotiating freeway traffic and the rodent dodging predators. Lewis Mumford observes that the uniform grid pattern of our cities "makes strangers as much at home as the oldest inhabitants." Americans who have become dependent on this pattern are often frustrated by anything different. It is difficult for them to feel at home in European capitals that don't conform to this simple plan. Those who travel and live abroad frequently get lost. An interesting feature of these complaints reveals the relationship of the layout to the person. Almost without exception, the newcomer uses words and tones associated with a personal affront, as though the town held something against him. It is no wonder that people brought up on either the French radiating star or the Roman grid have difficulty in a place like Japan where the entire fixed-feature pattern is basically and radically different. In fact, if one were to set out to design two systems in contrasts, it is hard to see how one could do better. The European systems stress the lines, which they name; the Japanese treat the intersecting points technically and forget about the lines. In Japan, the intersections but not the streets are named. Houses instead of being related in space are related in time and numbered in the order in which they are built. The Japanese pattern emphasizes hierarchies that grow around centers; the American plan finds its ultimate development in the sameness of suburbia, because one number along a line is the same as any other. In a Japanese neighborhood, the first house built is a constant reminder to the residents of house #20 that #1 was there first.

Some aspects of fixed-feature space are not visible until one observes human behavior. For example, although the separate dining room is fast vanishing from American houses, the line separating the dining area from the rest of the living room is quite real. The invisible boundary which separates one yard from another in suburbia is also a fixed-feature of American culture or at least some of its subcultures.

Architects traditionally are preoccupied with the visual patterns of structures—what one sees. They are almost totally unaware of the fact that people carry around with them internalizations of fixed-feature space learned early in life. It isn't only the Arab who feels depressed unless he has enough space but many Americans as well. As one of my subjects said: "I can put up with almost anything as long as I have large rooms and high ceilings. You see, I was raised in an old house in Brooklyn and I have never been able to accustom myself to anything different." Fortunately, there are a few architects who take the time to discover the internalized fixed-feature needs of their clients. However, the *individual* client is not my primary concern. The problem facing us today in designing and rebuilding our cities is understanding the needs of large numbers of people. We are building huge apartment houses and mammoth office buildings with no understanding of the needs of the occupants.

The important point about fixed-feature space is that it is the mold into which a great deal of behavior is cast. It was this feature of space that the late Sir Winston Churchill referred to when he said: "We shape our buildings and they shape us." During the debate on restoring the House of Commons after the war, Churchill feared that departure from the intimate spatial pattern of the House, where opponents face each other across a narrow aisle, would seriously alter the patterns of government. He may not have been the first to put his finger on the influence of fixed-feature space, but its effects have never been so succinctly stated.

One of the many basic differences between cultures is that they extend different anatomical and behavioral features of the human organism. Whenever there is cross-cultural borrowing, the borrowed items have to be adapted. Otherwise, the new and the old do not match, and in some instances, the two patterns are completely contradictory. For example, Japan has had problems integrating the automobile into a culture in which the lines between points (highways) receive less attention than the points. Hence, Tokyo is famous for producing some of the world's most impressive traffic jams. The automobile is also poorly adapted to India, where cities are physically crowded and the society has elaborate hierarchical features. Unless Indian engineers can design roads that will separate slow pedestrians from fast-moving vehicles, the class-conscious drivers' lack of consideration for the poor will continue to breed disaster. Even Le Corbusier's great buildings at Chandigarh, capital of Punjab, had to be modified by the residents to make them habitable. The Indians walled up Corbusier's balconies, converting them into kitchens! Similarly, Arabs coming to the United States find that their own internalized fixed-feature patterns do not fit American housing. Arabs feel oppressed by it—the ceilings are too low, the rooms too small, privacy from the outside inadequate, and views non-existent.

It should not be thought, however, that incongruity between internalized and externalized patterns occurs only between cultures. As our own technology explodes, air conditioning, fluorescent lighting, and soundproofing make it possible to design houses and offices without regard to traditional patterns of windows and doors. The new inventions sometimes result in great barnlike rooms where the "territory" of scores of employees in a "bull pen" is ambiguous.

SEMIFIXED-FEATURE SPACE

Several years ago, a talented and perceptive physician named Humphry Osmond was asked to direct a large health and research center in Saskatchewan. His hospital was one of the first in which the relationship between semifixed-feature space and behavior was clearly demonstrated. Osmond had noticed that some spaces, like railway waiting rooms, tend to keep people apart. These he called sociofugal spaces. Others, such as the booths in the old-fashioned drugstore or the tables at a French sidewalk café, tend to bring people together. These he called sociopetal. The hospital of which he was in charge was replete with sociofugal spaces and had very few which might be called sociopetal. Furthermore, the custodial staff and nurses tended to prefer the former to the latter because they were easier to maintain. Chairs in the halls, which would be found in little circles after visiting hours, would soon be lined up neatly in military fashion, in rows along the walls.

One situation which attracted Osmond's attention was the newly built "model" female geriatrics ward. Everything was new and shiny, neat and clean. There was enough space, and the colors were cheerful. The only trouble was that the longer the patients stayed in the ward, the less they seemed to talk to each other. Gradually, they were becoming like the furniture, permanently and silently glued to the walls at regular intervals between the beds. In addition, they all seemed depressed.

Sensing that the space was more sociofugal than sociopetal, Osmond put a perceptive young psychologist, Robert Sommer, to work to find out as much as he could about the relationship of furniture to conversations. Looking for a natural setting which offered a number of different situations in which people could be observed in conversations, Sommer selected the hospital cafeteria, where 36 by 72-inch tables accommodated six people. As the figure below indicates, these tables provided six different distances and orientations of the bodies in relation to each other.

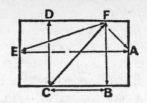

F–A Across the corner
C–B Side by side
C–D Across the table
E–A From one end to the other
E–F Diagonally the length of the table
C–F Diagonally across the table

Fifty observational sessions in which conversations were counted at controlled intervals revealed that: *F–A* (cross corner) conversations were twice as frequent as the *C–B* (side by side) type, which in turn were three times as frequent as those at *C–D* (across the table). No conversations were observed by Sommer for the other positions. In other words, corner situations with people at right angles to each other produced six times as many conversations as face-to-face situations across the 36-inch span of the table, and twice as many as the side-by-side arrangement.

The results of these observations suggested a solution to the problem of gradual disengagement and withdrawal of the old people. But before anything could be done, a number of preparations had to be made. As everyone knows, people have deep personal feelings about space and furniture arrangements. Neither the staff nor the patients would put up with outsiders "messing around" with their furniture. Osmond, as director, could order anything he wanted done, but he knew the staff would quietly sabotage any arbitrary moves. So the first step was to involve them in a series of "experiments." Both Osmond and Sommer had noted that the ward patients were more often in the *B–C* and *C–D* relationships (side by side and across) than they were in the cafeteria, and they sat at much greater distances. In addition, there was no place to put anything, no place for personal belongings. The only territorial features associated with the patients were the bed and the chair. As a consequence, magazines ended up on the floor and were quickly swept up by staff members. Enough small tables so that every patient had a place would provide additional territoriality and an opportunity to keep magazines, books, and writing materials. If the tables were square, they would also help to structure relationships between patients so that there was a maximum opportunity to converse.

Once the staff had been cajoled into participating in the experiments, the small tables were moved in and the chairs arranged around them. At first, the patients resisted. They had become accustomed to the placement of "their" chairs in particular spots, and they did not take easily to being moved around by others. By now, the staff was involved to the point of keeping the new arrangement reasonably intact until it was established as an alternative rather than an annoying feature to be selectively inattended. When this point had been reached, a repeat count of conversations was made. The number of conversations had doubled, while reading had tripled, possibly because there was now a place to keep reading material. Similar restructuring of the dayroom met with the same resistances and the same ultimate increase in verbal interaction.

At this point, three things must be said. Conclusions drawn from observations made in the hospital situation just described are not universally applicable. That is, across-the-corner-at-right-angles is conducive *only* to: (a) conversations of certain types between (b) persons in certain relationships and (c) in very restricted cultural settings. Second, what is sociofugal in one culture may be sociopetal in another. Third, sociofugal space is not necessarily bad, nor is sociopetal space universally good. What *is* desirable is flexibility and congruence between design and function so that there is a variety of spaces, and people can be involved or not, as the occasion and mood demand. The main point of the Canadian experiment for us is its demonstration that the structuring of semifixed-features can have a profound effect on behavior and that this effect is measurable. This will come as no surprise to housewives who are constantly trying to balance the relationship of fixed-feature enclosures to arrangement of their semifixed furniture. Many have had the experience of getting a room nicely arranged, only to find that conversation was impossible if the chairs were left nicely arranged.

It should be noted that what is fixed-feature space in one culture may be semifixed in another, and vice versa. In Japan, for example, the walls are movable, opening and closing as the day's activities change. In the United States, people move from room to room or from one part of a room to another for each different activity, such as eating, sleeping, working, or socializing with relatives. In Japan, it is quite common for the person to remain in one spot while the activities change. The Chinese provide us with further opportunities to observe the diversity of human treatment of space, for they assign to the fixed-feature category certain items which Americans treat as semifixed. Apparently, a guest in a Chinese home *does not move his chair* except at the host's suggestion. To do so would be like going into someone else's home and moving a screen or even a partition. In this sense, the semifixed nature of furniture in American homes is merely a matter of degree and situation. Light chairs are more mobile than sofas or heavy tables. I have noted, however, that some Americans hesitate to adjust furniture in another person's house or office. Of the forty students in one of my classes, half manifested such hesitation.

Many American women know it is hard to find things in someone else's kitchen. Conversely, it can be exasperating to have kitchenware put away by well-meaning helpers who don't know where things "belong." How and where belongings are arranged and stored is a function of microcultural patterns, representative not only of large cultural groups but of the minute variations on cultures that make each individual unique. Just as variations in the quality and use of the voice make it possible to distinguish one person's voice from another, handling of materials also has a characteristic pattern that is unique.

INFORMAL SPACE

We turn now to the category of spatial experience, which is perhaps most significant for the individual because it includes the distances maintained in encounters with others. These distances are for the most part outside awareness. I have called this category *informal space* because it is unstated, not because it lacks form or has no importance. Indeed, as the next chapter will show, informal spatial patterns have distinct bounds, and such deep, if unvoiced, significance that they form an essential part of the culture. To misunderstand this significance may invite disaster.

X

DISTANCES IN MAN

Some thirty inches from my nose
The frontier of my Person goes,
And all the untilled air between
Is private *pagus* or demesne.
Stranger, unless with bedroom eyes
I beckon you to fraternize,
Beware of rudely crossing it:
I have no gun, but I can spit.
                        W. H. AUDEN
                        "Prologue:
                        The Birth of Architecture"

Birds and mammals not only have territories which they
occupy and defend against their own kind but they have a
series of uniform distances which they maintain from each
other. Hediger has classified these as flight distance, critical
distance, and personal and social distance. Man, too, has a
uniform way of handling distance from the fellows. With very
few exceptions, flight distance and critical distance have been
eliminated from human reactions. Personal distance and social distance, however, are obviously still present.

How many distances do human beings have and how do we
distinguish them? What is it that differentiates one distance
from the other? The answer to this question was not obvious
at first when I began my investigation of distances in man.
Gradually, however, evidence began to accumulate indicating
that the regularity of distances observed for humans is the
consequence of sensory shifts—the type cited in Chapters VII
and VIII.

One common source of information about the distance

separating two people is the loudness of the voice. Working with the linguistic scientist George Trager, I began by observing shifts in the voice associated with changes in distance. Since the whisper is used when people are very close, and the shout is used to span great distances, the question Trager and I posed was, How many vocal shifts are sandwiched between these two extremes? Our procedure for discovering these patterns was for Trager to stand still while I talked to him at different distances. If both of us agreed that a vocal shift had occurred, we would then measure the distance and note down a general description. The result was the eight distances described at the end of Chapter Ten in *The Silent Language*.

Further observation of human beings in social situations convinced me that these eight distances were overly complex. Four were sufficient; these I have termed intimate, personal, social, and public (each with its close and far phase). My choice of terms to describe various distances was deliberate. Not only was it influenced by Hediger's work with animals indicating the continuity between *infra*culture and culture but also by a desire to provide a clue as to the types of activities and relationships associated with each distance, thereby linking them in peoples' minds with specific inventories of relationships and activities. It should be noted at this point that *how people are feeling toward each other* at the time is a decisive factor in the distance used. Thus people who are very angry or emphatic about the point they are making will move in close, they "turn up the volume," as it were, by shouting. Similarly—as any woman knows—one of the first signs that a man is beginning to feel amorous is his move closer to her. If the woman does not feel similarly disposed she signals this by moving back.

THE DYNAMISM OF SPACE

In Chapter VII we saw that man's sense of space and distance is not static, that it has very little to do with the single-viewpoint linear perspective developed by the Renaissance artists and still taught in most schools of art and architecture.

Instead, man senses distance as other animals do. His perception of space is dynamic because it is related to action—what can be done in a given space—rather than what is seen by passive viewing.

The general failure to grasp the significance of the many elements that contribute to man's sense of space may be due to two mistaken notions: (1) that for every effect there is a single and identifiable cause; and (2) that man's boundary begins and ends with his skin. If we can rid ourselves of the need for a single explanation, and if we can think of man as surrounded by a series of expanding and contracting fields which provide information of many kinds, we shall begin to see him in an entirely different light. We can then begin to learn about human behavior, including personality types. Not only are there introverts and extroverts, authoritarian and egalitarian, Apollonian and Dionysian types and all the other shades and grades of personality, but each one of us has a number of learned *situational* personalities. The simplest form of the situational personality is that associated with responses to intimate, personal, social, and public transactions. Some individuals never develop the public phase of their personalities and, therefore, cannot fill public spaces; they make very poor speakers or moderators. As many psychiatrists know, other people have trouble with the intimate and personal zones and cannot endure closeness to others.

Concepts such as these are not always easy to grasp, because most of the distance-sensing process occurs outside awareness. We sense other people as close or distant, but we cannot always put our finger on what it is that enables us to characterize them as such. So many different things are happening at once it is difficult to sort out the sources of information on which we base our reactions. Is it tone of voice or stance or distance? This sorting process can be accomplished only by careful observation over a long period of time in a wide variety of situations, making a note of each small shift in information received. For example, the presence or absence of the sensation of warmth from the body of another person marks the line between intimate and non-intimate space. The smell of freshly washed hair and the blurring of another person's features seen close up combine with the sensation of warmth to create intimacy. By using one's self as a control and recording changing patterns of sensory input it is possible to identify structure points in the distance-sensing system. In effect, one identifies, one by one, the isolates making up the sets that constitute the intimate, personal, social, and public zones.

The following descriptions of the four distance zones have been compiled from observations and interviews with non-contact, middle-class, healthy adults, mainly natives of the northeastern seaboard of the United States. A high percentage of the subjects were men and women from business and the professions; many could be classified as intellectuals. The interviews were effectively neutral; that is, the subjects were not noticeably excited, depressed, or angry. There were no unusual environmental factors, such as extremes of temperature or noise. These descriptions represent only a first approximation. They will doubtless seem crude when more is known about proxemic observation and how people distinguish one distance from another. It should be emphasized that these generalizations are not representative of human behavior in general—or even of American behavior in general —but only of the group included in the sample. Negroes and Spanish Americans as well as persons who come from southern European cultures have very different proxemic patterns.

Each of the four distance zones described below has a near and a far phase, which will be discussed after short introductory remarks. It should be noted that the measured distances vary somewhat with differences in personality and environmental factors. For example, a high noise level or low illumination will ordinarily bring people closer together.

INTIMATE DISTANCE

At intimate distance, the presence of the other person is unmistakable and may at times be overwhelming because of the greatly stepped-up sensory inputs. Sight (often distorted), olfaction, heat from the other person's body, sound, smell, and feel of the breath all combine to signal unmistakable involvement with another body.

Intimate Distance—Close Phase

This is the distance of love-making and wrestling, comforting and protecting. Physical contact or the high possibility of physical involvement is uppermost in the awareness of both persons. The use of their distance receptors is greatly reduced except for olfaction and sensation of radiant heat, both of which are stepped up. In the maximum contact phase, the muscles and skin communicate. Pelvis, thighs, and head can be brought into play; arms can encircle. Except at the outer limits, sharp vision is blurred. When close vision is possible within the intimate range—as with children—the image is greatly enlarged and stimulates much, if not all, of the retina. The detail that can be seen at this distance is extraordinary. This detail plus the cross-eyed pull of the eye muscles provide a visual experience that cannot be confused with any other distance. Vocalization at intimate distance plays a very minor part in the communication process, which is carried mainly by other channels. A whisper has the effect of expanding the distance. The vocalizations that do occur are largely involuntary.

Intimate Distance—Far Phase

(Distance: six to eighteen inches)
Heads, thighs, and pelvis are not easily brought into contact, but hands can reach and grasp extremities. The head is seen as enlarged in size, and its features are distorted. Ability to focus the eye easily is an important feature of this distance for Americans. The iris of the other person's eye seen at about six to nine inches is enlarged to more than life-size. Small blood vessels in the sclera are clearly perceived, pores are enlarged. Clear vision (15 degrees) includes the upper or lower portion of the face, which is perceived as enlarged. The nose is seen as over-large and may look distorted, as will other features such as lips, teeth, and tongue. Peripheral vision (30 to 180 degrees) includes the outline of head and shoulders and very often the hands.

Much of the physical discomfort that Americans experience

when foreigners are inappropriately inside the intimate sphere is expressed as a distortion of the visual system. One subject said, "These people get so close, you're cross-eyed. It really makes me nervous. They put their face so close it feels like they're *inside you*." At the point where sharp focus is lost, one feels the uncomfortable muscular sensation of being cross-eyed from looking at something too close. The expressions "Get your face *out* of mine" and "He shook his fist *in* my face" apparently express how many Americans perceive their body boundaries.

At six to eighteen inches the voice is used but is normally held at a very low level or even a whisper. As Martin Joos, the linguist, describes it, "An intimate utterance pointedly avoids giving the addressee information from outside of the speaker's skin. The point . . . is simply to remind (hardly 'inform') the addressee of some feeling . . . inside the speaker's skin." The heat and odor of the other person's breath may be detected, even though it is directed away from subject's face. Heat loss or gain from other person's body begins to be noticed by some subjects.

The use of intimate distance in public is not considered proper by adult, middle-class Americans even though their young may be observed intimately involved with each other in automobiles and on beaches. Crowded subways and buses may bring strangers into what would ordinarily be classed as intimate spatial relations, but subway riders have defensive devices which take the real intimacy out of intimate space in public conveyances. The basic tactic is to be as immobile as possible and, when part of the trunk or extremities touches another person, withdraw if possible. If this is not possible, the muscles in the affected areas are kept tense. For members of the non-contact group, it is taboo to relax and enjoy bodily contact with strangers! In crowded elevators the hands are kept at the side or used to steady the body by grasping a railing. The eyes are fixed on infinity and are not brought to bear on anyone for more than a passing glance.

It should be noted once more that American proxemic patterns for intimate distance are by no means universal. Even the rules governing such intimacies as touching others cannot be counted on to remain constant. Americans who have had an opportunity for considerable social interaction with Russians report that many of the features characteristic of American intimate distance are present in Russian social distance. As we shall see in the following chapter, Middle Eastern subjects in public places do not express the outraged reaction to being touched by strangers which one encounters in American subjects.

PERSONAL DISTANCE

"Personal distance" is the term originally used by Hediger to designate the distance consistently separating the members of non-contact species. It might be thought of as a small protective sphere or bubble that an organism maintains between itself and others.

Personal Distance—Close Phase

(Distance: one and a half to two and a half feet)

The kinesthetic sense of closeness derives in part from the possibilities present in regard to what each participant can do to the other with his extremities. At this distance, one can hold or grasp the other person. Visual distortion of the other's features is no longer apparent. However, there is noticeable feedback from the muscles that control the eyes. The reader can experience this himself if he will look at an object eighteen inches to three feet away, paying particular attention to the muscles around his eyeballs. He can feel the pull of these muscles as they hold the two eyes on a single point so that the image of each eye stays in register. Pushing gently with the tip of the finger on the surface of the lower eyelid so that the eyeball is displaced will illustrate clearly the work these muscles perform in maintaining a single coherent image. A visual angle of 15 degrees takes in another person's upper or lower face, which is seen with exceptional clarity. The planes and roundness of the face are accentuated; the nose projects and the ears recede; fine hair of the face, eyelashes, and pores is clearly visible. The three-dimensional quality of objects is particularly pronounced. Objects have roundness, substance, and form unlike that perceived at any other distance. Surface textures are also very prominent and are clearly differentiated from each other. Where people stand in relation to each other signals their relationship, or how they feel toward each other, or both. A wife can stay inside the circle of her husband's close personal zone with impunity. For another woman to do so is an entirely different story.

Personal Distance—Far Phase

(Distance: two and a half to four feet)

Keeping someone at "arm's length" is one way of expressing the far phase of personal distance. It extends from a point that is just outside easy touching distance by one person to a point where two people can touch fingers if they extend both arms. This is the limit of physical domination in the very real sense. Beyond it, a person cannot easily "get his hands on" someone else. Subjects of personal interest and involvement can be discussed at this distance. Head size is perceived as normal and details of the other person's features are clearly visible. Also easily seen are fine details of skin, gray hair, "sleep" in the eye, stains on teeth, spots, small wrinkles, or dirt on clothing. Foveal vision covers only an area the size of the tip of the nose or one eye, so that the gaze must wander around the face (*where the eye is directed* is strictly a matter of cultural conditioning). Fifteen-degree clear vision covers the upper *or* lower face, while 180-degree peripheral vision takes in the hands and the whole body of a seated person. Movement of the hands is detected, but fingers can't be counted. The voice level is moderate. No body heat is perceptible. While olfaction is not normally present for Americans, it is for a great many other people who use colognes to create an olfactory bubble. Breath odor can sometimes be detected at this distance, but Americans are generally trained to direct the breath away from others.

SOCIAL DISTANCE

The boundary line between the far phase of personal distance and the close phase of social distance marks, in the words of one subject, the "limit of domination." Intimate visual detail in the face is not perceived, and nobody touches or expects to touch another person unless there is some special effort. Voice level is normal for Americans. There is little change between the far and close phases, and conversations can be overheard at a distance of up to twenty feet. I have observed that in overall loudness, the American voice at these distances is below that of the Arab, the Spaniard, the South Asian Indian, and the Russian, and somewhat above that of the English upper class, the Southeast Asian, and the Japanese.

Social Distance—Close Phase

(Distance: four to seven feet)

Head size is perceived as normal; as one moves away from the subject, the foveal area of the eye can take in an ever-increasing amount of the person. At four feet, a one-degree visual angle covers an area of a little more than one eye. At seven feet the area of sharp focus extends to the nose and parts of both eyes; or the whole mouth, one eye, and the nose are sharply seen. Many Americans shift their gaze back and forth from eye to eye or from eyes to mouth. Details of skin texture and hair are clearly perceived. At a 60-degree visual angle, the head, shoulders, and upper trunk are seen at a distance of four feet; while the same sweep includes the whole figure at seven feet.

Impersonal business occurs at this distance, and in the close phase there is more involvement than in the distant phase. People who work together tend to use close social distance. It is also a very common distance for people who are attending a casual social gathering. To stand and look down at a person at this distance has a domineering effect, as when a man talks to his secretary or receptionist.

Social Distance—Far Phase

(Distance: seven to twelve feet)

This is the distance to which people move when someone says, "Stand away so I can look at you." Business and social discourse conducted at the far end of social distance has a more formal character than if it occurs inside the close phase. Desks in the offices of important people are large enough to hold visitors at the far phase of social distance. Even in an office with standard-size desks, the chair opposite is eight or nine feet away from the man behind the desk. At the far phase of social distance, the finest details of the face, such as the capillaries in the eyes, are lost. Otherwise, skin texture, hair, condition of teeth, and condition of clothes are all readily visible. None of my subjects mentioned heat or odor from another person's body as detectable at this distance. The full figure—with a good deal of space around it—is encompassed in a 60-degree glance. Also, at around twelve feet, feedback from the eye muscles used to hold the eyes inward on a single spot falls off rapidly. The eyes and the mouth of the other person are seen in the area of sharpest vision. Hence, it is not necessary to shift the eyes to take in the whole face. During conversations of any significant length it is more important to maintain visual contact at this distance than it is at closer distance.

Proxemic behavior of this sort is culturally conditioned and entirely arbitrary. It is also binding on all concerned. To fail to hold the other person's eye is to shut him out and bring conversation to a halt, which is why people who are conversing at this distance can be observed craning their necks and leaning from side to side to avoid intervening obstacles. Similarly, when one person is seated and the other is standing, prolonged visual contact at less than ten or twelve feet tires the neck muscles and is generally avoided by subordinates who are sensitive to their employer's comfort. If, however, the status of the two parties is reversed so that the subordinate is seated, the other party may often come closer.

At this distant phase, the voice level is noticeably louder than for the close phase, and it can usually be heard easily in an adjoining room if the door is open. Raising the voice or shouting can have the effect of reducing social distance to personal distance.

A proxemic feature of social distance (far phase) is that it can be used to insulate or screen people from each other. This distance makes it possible for them to continue to work in the presence of another person without appearing to be rude. Receptionists in offices are particularly vulnerable as most employers expect double duty: answering questions, being polite to callers, as well as typing. If the receptionist is less than ten feet from another person, even a stranger, she will be sufficiently involved to be virtually compelled to converse. If she has more space, however, she can work quite freely without having to talk. Likewise, husbands returning from work often find themselves sitting and relaxing, reading the paper at ten or more feet from their wives, for at this distance a couple can engage each other briefly and disengage at will. Some men discover that their wives have arranged the furniture back-to-back—a favorite sociofugal device of the cartoonist Chick Young, creator of "Blondie." The back-to-back seating arrangement is an appropriate solution to minimum space because it is possible for two people to stay uninvolved if that is their desire.

PUBLIC DISTANCE

Several important sensory shifts occur in the transition from the personal and social distances to public distance, which is well outside the circle of involvement.

Public Distance—Close Phase

(Distance: twelve to twenty-five feet)

At twelve feet an alert subject can take evasive or defensive action if threatened. The distance may even cue a vestigial but subliminal form of flight reaction. The voice is loud but not full-volume. Linguists have observed that a careful choice of words and phrasing of sentences as well as grammatical or syntactic shifts occur at this distance. Martin Joos's choice of the term "formal style" is appropriately descriptive: "Formal texts . . . demand advance planning . . . the speaker is correctly said to think on his feet." The angle of sharpest vision (one degree) covers the whole face. Fine details of the skin and eyes are no longer visible. At sixteen feet, the body begins to lose its roundness and to look flat. The color of the eyes begins to be imperceivable; only the white of the eye is visible. Head size is perceived as considerably under life-size. The 15-degree lozenge-shaped area of clear vision covers the faces of two people at twelve feet, while 60-degree scanning includes the whole body with a little space around it. Other persons present can be seen peripherally.

Public Distance—Far Phase

(Distance: twenty-five feet or more)

Thirty feet is the distance that is automatically set around important public figures. An excellent example occurs in Theodore H. White's *The Making of the President 1960* when John F. Kennedy's nomination became a certainty. White is describing the group at the "hideaway cottage" as Kennedy entered:

> Kennedy loped into the cottage with his light, dancing step, as young and lithe as springtime, and called a greeting to those who stood in his way. Then he seemed to slip from them as he descended the steps of the split-level cottage to a corner where his brother Bobby and brother-in-law Sargent Shriver were chatting, waiting for him. The others in the room surged forward on impulse to join him. Then they halted. A distance of perhaps 30 feet separated them from him, but it was impassable. They stood apart, these older men of long-established power, and watched him. He turned after a few minutes, saw them watching him, and whispered to his brother-in-law. Shriver now crossed the separating space to invite them over. First Averell Harriman; then Dick Daley; then Mike DiSalle, then, one by one, let them all congratulate him. Yet no one could pass the little open distance between him and them uninvited, because there was this thin separation about him, and the knowledge they were there not as his patrons but as his clients. They

could come by invitation only, for this might be a President of the United States.

The usual public distance is not restricted to public figures but can be used by anyone on public occasions. There are certain adjustments that must be made, however. Most actors know that at thirty or more feet the subtle shades of meaning conveyed by the normal voice are lost as are the details of facial expression and movement. Not only the voice but everything else must be exaggerated or amplified. Much of the nonverbal part of the communication shifts to gestures and body stance. In addition, the tempo of the voice drops, words are enunciated more clearly, and there are stylistic changes as well. Martin Joos's *frozen style* is characteristic: "Frozen style is for people who are to remain strangers." The whole man may be seen as quite small and he is perceived in a setting. Foveal vision takes in more and more of the man until he is entirely within the small circle of sharpest vision. At which point—when people look like ants—contact with them as human beings fades rapidly. The 60-degree cone of vision takes in the setting while peripheral vision has as its principal function the altering of the individual to movement at the side.

WHY "FOUR" DISTANCES?

In concluding this description of distance zones common to our sample group of Americans a final word about classification is in order. It may well be asked: Why are there four zones, not six or eight? Why set up any zones at all? How do we know that this classification is appropriate? How were the categories chosen?

As I indicated earlier in Chapter VIII, the scientist has a basic need for a classification system, one that is as consistent as possible with the phenomena under observation and one which will hold up long enough to be useful. Behind every classification system lies a theory or hypothesis about the nature of the data and their basic patterns of organization. The hypothesis behind the proxemic classification system is this:

CHART SHOWING INTERPLAY OF THE DISTANT AND IMMEDIATE RECEPTORS
IN PROXEMIC PERCEPTION

FEET	0	1	2	3	4	5	6	7	8	10	12	14	16	18	20	22	30

INFORMAL DISTANCE CLASSIFICATION

INTIMATE — CLOSE / NOT CLOSE
PERSONAL — CLOSE, / NOT CLOSE
SOCIAL – CONSULTIVE — CLOSE / NOT CLOSE
PUBLIC

NOT CLOSE BEGINS AT 30' – 40'

MANDATORY RECOGNITION DISTANCE BEGINS HERE

KINESTHESIA

HEAD, PELVIS, THIGHS, TRUNK CAN BE BROUGHT INTO CONTACT OR MEMBERS CAN ACCIDENTALLY TOUCH.
HANDS CAN REACH & MANIPULATE ANY PART OF TRUNK EASILY.

HANDS CAN REACH AND HOLD EXTREMITIES EASILY BUT WITH MUCH LESS FACILITY THAN ABOVE. SEATED CAN REACH AROUND & TOUCH OTHER SIDE OF TRUNK. NOT SO CLOSE AS TO RESULT IN ACCIDENTAL TOUCHING.

ONE PERSON HAS ELBOW ROOM.

2 PEOPLE BARELY HAVE ELBOW ROOM. ONE CAN REACH OUT AND GRASP AN EXTREMITY.

JUST OUTSIDE TOUCHING DISTANCE.

OUT OF INTERFERENCE DISTANCE.
BY REACHING ONE CAN JUST TOUCH THE OTHER.

2 PEOPLE WHOSE HEADS ARE 8'–9' APART CAN PASS AN OBJECT BACK & FORTH BY BOTH STRETCHING.

THERMAL RECEPTORS — CONDUCTION (CONTACT)
RADIATION

NORMALLY OUT OF AWARENESS

ANIMAL HEAT AND MOISTURE DISSIPATE (THOREAU)

CULTURAL ATTITUDE

OLFACTION

WASHED SKIN & HAIR — OK
SHAVING LOTION—PERFUME — OK — TABOO
SEXUAL ODORS — VARIABLE — TABOO
BREATH — ANTISEPTIC OK, OTHERWISE TABOO
BODY ODOR — TABOO
FOOT ODOR — TABOO

FEET	0	1	2	3	4	5	6	7	8	10	12	14	16	18	20	22	30
VISION — DETAIL VISION (VIS ∠ OF FOVEA 1°)	DISTORTED VISION BLURRED	ENLARGED DETAILS OF IRIS, EYEBALL, PORES OF FACE, FINEST HAIRS	DETAIL OF FACE SEEN AT NORMAL SIZE, MOST SEVENTEETH CONTORTION, HAIR ON FACE OR NECK		SMALLEST BLOOD VESSELS IN EYE, VEINS, SEE WEAR ON CLOTHING, HELD HAIR SEEN CLEARLY		FINE LINES OF FACE FADE, DEEP LINES STAND OUT, SLIGHT EYE WINK, LIP MOVEMENT SEEN CLEARLY				ENTIRE CENTRAL FACE INCLUDED		SHARP FEATURES DISSOLVE, EYE COLOR NOT DISCERNING, SMILE-SCOWL VISIBLE, BLURRED JOINING MORE PRONOUNCED				SNELLEN'S STANDARD FOR DISTANT VISION · EMPLOYING ANGLE OF 1 MIN., QUID OPTICIANS OF AMERICA EYE CHART · A PERSON WITH 20/20 VISION HAS TROUBLE SEEING EYES EXPRESSION AROUND 22'. 6'3" x 11'7"
CLEAR VISION (VIS ∠ AT MACULA 12° HOR, 3° VERT)		39" x 9" ON EYE AREA, NOSTRIL ON MOUTH	5.25" .54" UPPER OR LOWER FACE	6.25" x 1.60" UPPER OR LOWER FACE	10" x 2.5" UPPER OR LOWER FACE		UPPER OR LOWER FACE OR SHOULDERS	20" x 5" 1 OR 2 FACES			31" x 7.5 FACES OF TWO PEOPLE		4'2" x 1'0" TORSOS OF TWO PEOPLE			6'3" x 11'7" TORSOS OF 4 OR 5 PEOPLE
60° SCANNING		1/2 OF FACE, NOSE PROJECTS, EYE CAN'T SEE MOUTH AREA, FACE DISTORTED	UPPER BODY CAN'T COUNT FINGERS		UPPER BODY & GESTURES		WHOLE SEATED BODY VISIBLE, PEOPLE OFTEN KEEP FEET WITHIN OTHER PERSON'S 60° ANGLE OF VIEW				WHOLE BODY HAS SPACE AROUND IT, POSTURAL COMMUNICATION BEGINS TO ASSUME IMPORTANCE					
PERIPHERAL VISION		HEAD AGAINST BACK-GROUND	HEAD & SHOULDERS	WHOLE BODY MOVEMENT IN HANDS, FINGERS VISIBLE	WHOLE BODY		OTHER PEOPLE SEEN IF PRESENT						OTHER PEOPLE BECOME IMPORTANT IN PERIPHERAL VISION			
HEAD SIZE		FILLS VISUAL FIELD FAR OVER LIFE SIZE	OVER NORMAL	NORMAL SIZE			NOTE: PERCEIVED HEAD SIZE VARIES EVEN WITH SAME SUBJECT AND DISTANCE		NORMAL TO BEGINNING TO SHRINK				VERY SMALL			
ADDITIONAL NOTES		SENSATION OF BEING CROSS-EYED								PEOPLE & OBJECTS SEEN AS ROUND UP TO 12'-15'			ACCOMMODATIVE CONVERGENCE ENDS AFTER 15' PEOPLE & OBJECTS BEGIN TO FLATTEN OUT			
TASKS IN SUBMARINES		67% OF TASKS IN THIS RANGE	23% FALL IN THIS RANGE						DIMMICK, F.L, & FARNSWORTH, 3, VISUAL ACUITY TASKS IN A SUBMARINE, NEW LONDON, 1951							
ARTIST'S OBSERVATIONS CF GROSSER		VERY PERSONAL DISTANCE	ARTIST OR MODEL HAS TO DOMINATE		A PORTRAIT, A PICTURE PAINTED AT 4 - 8' OF A PERSON WHO, IS NOT SAID TO "SIT"			TOO FAR FOR A CONVERSATION			BODY IS 1/3 SIZE		FULL LENGTH STATE PORTRAITS; HUMAN BODY SEEN AS A WHOLE, COMPREHENDED AT A GLANCE, WARMTH AND IDENTIFICATION CEASE			
ORAL / AURAL	GRUNTS GROANS	WHISPER — SOFT VOICE	CONVENTIONAL MODIFIED VOICE						LOUD VOICE WHEN TALKING TO A GROUP, MUST RAISE VOICE TO GET ATTENTION				FULL PUBLIC SPEAKING VOICE			
		INTIMATE STYLE	CASUAL OR CONSULTATIVE STYLE						FORMAL STYLE				FROZEN STYLE			

NOTE: THE BOUNDARIES ASSOCIATED WITH THE TRANSITION FROM ONE VOICE LEVEL TO THE NEXT HAVE NOT BEEN PRECISELY DETERMINED it is in the nature of animals, including man, to exhibit behavior which we call territoriality. In so doing, they use the senses to distinguish between one space or distance and another. The specific distance chosen depends on the transaction; the relationship of the interacting individuals, how they feel, and what they are doing. The four-part classification system used here is based on observations of both animals and men. Birds and apes exhibit intimate, personal, and social distances just as man does.

Western man has combined consultative and social activities and relationships into one distance set and has added the public figure and the public relationship. "Public" relations and "public" manners as the Europeans and Americans practice them are different from those in other parts of the world. There are implicit obligations to treat total strangers in certain prescribed ways. Hence, we find four principal categories of relationships (intimate, personal, social, and public) and the activities and spaces associated with them. In other parts of the world, relationships tend to fall into other patterns, such as the family/non-family pattern common in Spain and Portugal and their former colonies or the caste and outcast system of India. Both the Arabs and the Jews also make sharp distinctions between people to whom they are related and those to whom they are not. My work with Arabs leads me to believe that they employ a system for the organization of informal space which is very different from what I observed in the United States. The relationship of the Arab peasant or fellah to his sheik or to God is not a public relationship. It is close and personal without intermediaries.

Until recently man's space requirements were thought of in terms of the actual amount of air displaced by his body. The fact that man has around him as extensions of his personality the zones described earlier has generally been overlooked. Differences in the zones—in fact their very existence—became apparent only when Americans began interacting with foreigners who organize their senses differently so that what was intimate in one culture might be personal or even public in another. Thus for the first time the American became aware of his own spatial envelopes, which he had previously taken for granted.

The ability to recognize these various zones of involvement and the activities, relationships, and emotions associated with each has now become extremely important. The world's populations are crowding into cities, and builders and speculators are packing people into vertical filing boxes—both offices and dwellings. If one looks at human beings in the way that the early slave traders did, conceiving of their space requirements simply in terms of the limits of the body, one pays very little attention to the effects of crowding. If, however, one sees man surrounded by a series of invisible bubbles which have measurable dimensions, architecture can be seen in a new light. It is then possible to conceive that people can be cramped by the spaces in which they have to live and work. They may even find themselves forced into behavior, relationships, or emotional outlets that are overly stressful. Like gravity, the influence of two bodies on each other is inversely proportional not only to the square of the distance but possibly even the cube of the distance between them. When stress increases, sensitivity to crowding rises—people get more on edge—so that more and more space is required as less and less is available.

The next two chapters, dealing with proxemic patterns for people of different cultures, are designed to serve a double purpose: first, to shed additional light on our own out-of-awareness patterns and by this means hopefully to contribute to improved design of living and working structures and cities as well; and second, to show the great need for improved intercultural understanding. Proxemic patterns point up in sharp contrast some of the basic differences between people —differences which can be ignored only at great risk. American city planners and builders are now in the process of designing cities in other countries with very little idea of people's spatial needs and practically no inkling that these needs vary from culture to culture. The chances of forcing whole populations into molds that do not fit are very great indeed. Within the United States urban renewal and the many crimes against humanity that are committed in its name usually demonstrate total ignorance of how to create congenial environments for the diverse populations that are pouring into our cities.

XI

PROXEMICS IN A CROSS-CULTURAL CONTEXT: GERMANS, ENGLISH, AND FRENCH

The Germans, the English, the Americans, and the French share significant portions of each other's cultures, but at many points their cultures clash. Consequently, the misunderstandings that arise are all the more serious because sophisticated Americans and Europeans take pride in correctly interpreting each other's behavior. Cultural differences which are out of awareness are, as a consequence, usually chalked up to ineptness, boorishness, or lack of interest on the part of the other person.

THE GERMANS

Whenever people from different countries come into repeated contact they begin to generalize about each other's behavior. The Germans and the German Swiss are no exception. Most of the intellectual and professional people I have talked to from these two countries eventually get around to commenting on American use of time and space. Both the Germans and the German Swiss have made consistent observations about how Americans structure time very tightly and are sticklers for schedules. They also note that Americans don't leave any free time for themselves (a point which has been made by Sebastian de Grazia in *Of Time, Work, and Leisure*).

Since neither the Germans nor the Swiss (particularly the German Swiss) could be regarded as completely casual about time, I have made it a point to question them further about their view of the American approach to time. They will say that Europeans will schedule fewer events in the same time than Americans do and they usually add that Europeans feel less "pressed" for time than Americans. Certainly, Europeans allow more time for virtually everything involving important human relationships. Many of my European subjects observed that in Europe human relationships are important whereas in the United States the schedule is important. Several of my subjects then took the next logical step and connected the handling of time with attitudes toward space, which Americans treat with incredible casualness. According to European standards, Americans use space in a wasteful way and seldom plan adequately for public needs. In fact, it would seem that Americans feel that people have no needs associated with space at all. By overemphasizing the schedule Americans tend to underemphasize individual space needs. I should mention at this point that all Europeans are not this perceptive. Many of them go no further than to say that in the United States they themselves feel pressured by time and they often complain that our cities lack variety. Nevertheless, given these observations made by Europeans one would expect that the Germans would be more upset by violations of spatial mores than the Americans.

Germans and Intrusions

I shall never forget my first experience with German proxemic patterns, which occurred when I was an undergraduate. My manners, my status, and my ego were attacked and crushed by a German in an instance where thirty years' residence in this country and an excellent command of English had not attenuated German definitions of what constitutes an intrusion. In order to understand the various issues that were at stake, it is necessary to refer back to two basic American patterns that are taken for granted in this country and which Americans therefore tend to treat as universal.

First, in the United States there is a commonly accepted, invisible boundary around any two or three people in conversation which separates them from others. Distance alone serves to isolate any such group and to endow it with a protective wall of privacy. Normally, voices are kept low to avoid intruding on others and if voices are heard, people will act as though they had not heard. In this way, privacy is granted whether it is actually present or not. The second pattern is somewhat more subtle and has to do with the exact point at which a person is experienced as actually having crossed a boundary and entered a room. Talking through a screen door while standing outside a house is not considered by most Americans as being inside the house or room in any sense of the word. If one is standing on the threshold holding the door open and talking to someone inside, it is still defined informally and experienced as being *outside*. If one is in an office building and just "pokes his head in the door" of an office he's still outside the office. Just holding on to the doorjamb when one's body is inside the room still means a person has one foot "on base" as it were so that he is not quite inside the other fellow's territory. None of these American spatial definitions is valid in northern Germany. In every instance where the American would consider himself *outside* he has already entered the German's territory and by definition would become involved with him. The following experience brought the conflict between these two patterns into focus.

It was a warm spring day of the type one finds only in the high, clean, clear air of Colorado, the kind of day that makes you glad you are alive. I was standing on the doorstep of a converted carriage house talking to a young woman who lived in an apartment upstairs. The first floor had been made into an artist's studio. The arrangement, however, was peculiar because the same entrance served both tenants. The occupants of the apartment used a small entryway and walked along one wall of the studio to reach the stairs to the apartment. You might say that they had an "easement" through the artist's territory. As I stood talking on the doorstep, I glanced to the left and noticed that some fifty to sixty feet away, inside the studio, the Prussian artist and two of his friends were also in conversation. He was facing so that if he glanced to one side he could just see me. I had noted his presence, but not wanting to appear presumptuous or to interrupt his conversation, I unconsciously applied the American rule and assumed that the two activities—my quiet conversation and his conversation—were not involved with each other. As I was soon to learn, this was a mistake, because in less time than it takes to tell, the artist had detached himself from his friends, crossed the intervening space, pushed my friend aside, and with eyes flashing, started shouting at me. By what right had I entered his studio without greeting him? Who had given me permission?

I felt bullied and humiliated, and even after almost thirty years, I can still feel my anger. Later study has given me greater understanding of the German pattern and I have learned that in the German's eyes I really had been intolerably rude. I was already "inside" the building and I intruded when I could *see* inside. For the German, there is no such thing as being inside the room without being inside the zone of intrusion, particularly if one looks at the other party, no matter how far away.

Recently, I obtained an independent check on how Germans feel about visual intrusion while investigating what people look at when they are in intimate, personal, social, and public situations. In the course of my research, I instructed subjects to photograph separately both a man and a woman in each of the above contexts. One of my assistants, who also happened to be German, photographed his subjects out of focus at public distance because, as he said, "You are not really supposed to look at other people at public distances *because it's intruding*." This may explain the informal custom behind the German laws against photographing strangers in public without their permission.

The "Private Sphere"

Germans sense their own space as an extension of the ego. One sees a clue to this feeling in the term "Lebensraum," which is impossible to translate because it summarizes so much. Hitler used it as an effective psychological lever to move the Germans to conquest.

In contrast to the Arab, as we shall see later, the German's ego is extraordinarily exposed, and he will go to almost any length to preserve his "private sphere." This was observed during World War II when American soldiers were offered opportunities to observe German prisoners under a variety of circumstances. In one instance in the Midwest, German P.W.s were housed four to a small hut. As soon as materials were available, each prisoner built a partition so that he could have *his own space*. In a less favorable setting in Germany when the *Wehrmacht* was collapsing, it was necessary to use open stockades because German prisoners were arriving faster than they could be accommodated. In this situation each soldier who could find the materials built his own tiny dwelling unit, sometimes no larger than a foxhole. It puzzled the Americans that the Germans did not pool their efforts and their scarce materials to create a larger, more efficient space, particularly in view of the very cold spring nights. Since that time I have observed frequent instances of the use of architectural extensions of this need to screen the ego. German houses with balconies are arranged so that there is visual privacy. Yards tend to be well fenced; but fenced or not, they are sacred.

The American view that space should be shared is particularly troublesome to the German. I cannot document the account of the early days of World War II occupation when Berlin was in ruins but the following situation was reported by an observer and it has the nightmarish quality that is often associated with inadvertent cross-cultural blunders. In Berlin at that time the housing shortage was indescribably acute. To provide relief, occupation authorities in the American zone ordered those Berliners who still had kitchens and baths intact to share them with their neighbors. The order finally had to be rescinded when the already overstressed Germans started killing each other over the shared facilities.

Public and private buildings in Germany often have double doors for soundproofing, as do many hotel rooms. In addition, the door is taken very seriously by Germans. Those Germans who come to America feel that our doors are flimsy and light. The meanings of the open door and the closed door are quite different in the two countries. In offices, Americans keep doors open; Germans keep doors closed. In Germany, the closed door does not mean that the man behind it wants to be alone or undisturbed, or that he is doing something he doesn't want someone else to see. It's simply that Germans think that open doors are sloppy and disorderly.

To close the door preserves the integrity of the room and provides a protective boundary between people. Otherwise, they get too involved with each other. One of my German subjects commented, "If our family hadn't had doors, we would have had to change our way of life. Without doors we would have had many, many more fights. . . . When you can't talk, you retreat behind a door. . . . If there hadn't been doors, I would always have been within reach of my mother."

Whenever a German warms up to the subject of American enclosed space, he can be counted on to comment on the noise that is transmitted through walls and doors. To many Germans, our doors epitomize American life. They are thin and cheap; they seldom fit; and they lack the substantial quality of German doors. When they close they don't sound and feel solid. The click of the lock is indistinct, it rattles and indeed it may even be absent.

The open-door policy of American business and the closed-door patterns of German business culture cause clashes in the branches and subsidiaries of American firms in Germany. The point seems to be quite simple, yet failure to grasp it has caused considerable friction and misunderstanding between American and German managers overseas. I was once called in to advise a firm that has operations all over the world. One of the first questions asked was, "How do you get the Germans to keep their doors open?" In this company the open doors were making the Germans feel exposed and gave the whole operation an unusually relaxed and unbusinesslike air. Closed doors, on the other hand, gave the Americans the feeling that there was a conspiratorial air about the place and that they were being left out. The point is that whether the door is open or shut, it is not going to mean the same thing in the two countries.

Order in Space

The orderliness and hierarchical quality of German culture are communicated in their handling of space. Germans want to know where they stand and object strenuously to people crashing queues or people who "get out of line" or who do not obey signs such as "Keep out," "Authorized personnel only," and the like. Some of the German attitudes toward ourselves are traceable to our informal attitudes toward boundaries and to authority in general.

However, German anxiety due to American violations of order is nothing compared to that engendered in Germans by the Poles, who see no harm in a little disorder. To them lines and queues stand for regimentation and blind authority. I once saw a Pole crash a cafeteria line just "to stir up those sheep."

Germans get very technical about intrusion distance, as I mentioned earlier. When I once asked my students to describe the distance at which a third party would intrude on two people who were talking, there were no answers from the Americans. Each student knew that he could tell when he was being intruded on but he couldn't define intrusion or tell how he knew when it had occurred. However, a German and an Italian who had worked in Germany were both members of my class and they answered without any hesitation. Both stated that a third party would intrude on two people if he came within seven feet!

Many Americans feel that Germans are overly rigid in their behavior, unbending and formal. Some of this impression is created by differences in the handling of chairs while seated. The American doesn't seem to mind if people hitch their chairs up to adjust the distance to the situation—those that do mind would not think of saying anything, for to comment on the manners of others would be impolite. In Germany, however, it is a violation of the mores to change the position of your chair. An added deterrent for those who don't know better is the weight of most German furniture. Even the great architect Mies van der Rohe, who often rebelled against German tradition in his buildings, made his handsome chairs so heavy that anyone but a strong man would have difficulty in adjusting his seating position. To a German, light furniture is anathema, not only because it seems flimsy but because people move it and thereby destroy the order of things, including intrusions on the "private sphere." In one instance reported to me, a German newspaper editor who had moved to the United States had his visitor's chair bolted to the floor "at the proper distance" because he couldn't tolerate the American habit of adjusting the chair to the situation.

THE ENGLISH

It has been said that the English and the Americans are two great people separated by one language. The differences for which language gets blamed may not be due so much to words as to communications on other levels beginning with English intonation (which sounds affected to many Americans) and continuing to ego-linked ways of handling time, space, and materials. If there ever were two cultures in which differences of the proxemic details are marked it is in the educated (public school) English and the middle-class Americans. One of the basic reasons for this wide disparity is that in the United States we use space as a way of classifying people and activities, whereas in England it is the social system that determines who you are. In the United States, your address is an important cue to status (this applies not only to one's home but to the business address as well). The Joneses from Brooklyn and Miami are not as "in" as the Joneses from Newport and Palm Beach. Greenwich and Cape Cod are worlds apart from Newark and Miami. Businesses located on Madison and Park avenues have more tone than those on Seventh and Eighth avenues. A corner office is more prestigious than one next to the elevator or at the end of a long hall. The Englishman, however, is born and brought up in a social system. He is still Lord — no matter where you find him, even if it is behind the counter in a fishmonger's stall. In addition to class distinctions, there are differences between the English and ourselves in how space is allotted.

The middle-class American growing up in the United States feels he has a right to have his own room, or at least part of a room. My American subjects, when asked to draw an ideal room or office, invariably drew it for themselves and no one else. When asked to draw their present room or office, they drew only their own part of a shared room and then drew a line down the middle. Both male and female subjects identified the kitchen and the master bedroom as belonging to the mother or the wife, whereas Father's territory was a study or a den, if one was available; otherwise, it was "the shop," "the basement," or sometimes only a workbench or the garage. American women who want to be alone can go to the bedroom and close the door. The closed door is the sign meaning "Do not disturb" or "I'm angry." An American is available if his door is open at home or at his office. He is expected not to shut himself off but to maintain himself in a state of constant readiness to answer the demands of others. Closed doors are for conferences, private conversations, and business, work that requires concentration, study, resting, sleeping, dressing, and sex.

The middle- and upper-class Englishman, on the other hand, is brought up in a nursery shared with brothers and sisters. The oldest occupies a room by himself which he vacates when he leaves for boarding school, possibly even at the age of nine or ten. The difference between a room of one's own and early conditioning to shared space, while seeming inconsequential, has an important effect on the Englishman's attitude toward his own space. He may never have a permanent "room of his own" and seldom expects one or feels he is entitled to one. Even Members of Parliament have no offices and often conduct their business on the terrace overlooking the Thames. As a consequence, the English are puzzled by the American need for a secure place in which to work, an office. Americans working in England may become annoyed if they are not provided with what they consider appropriate enclosed work space. In regard to the need for walls as a screen for the ego, this places the Americans somewhere between the Germans and the English.

The contrasting English and American patterns have some remarkable implications, particularly if we assume that man, like other animals, has a built-in need to shut himself off from others from time to time. An English student in one of my seminars typified what happens when hidden patterns clash. He was quite obviously experiencing strain in his relationships with Americans. Nothing seemed to go right and it was quite clear from his remarks that we did not know how to behave. An analysis of his complaints showed that a major source of irritation was that no American seemed to be able to pick up the subtle clues that there were times when he didn't want his thoughts intruded on. As he stated it, "I'm walking around the apartment and it seems that whenever I want to be alone my roommate starts talking to me. Pretty soon he's asking 'What's the matter?' and wants to know if I'm angry. By then I am angry and say something."

It took some time but finally we were able to identify most of the contrasting features of the American and British problems that were in conflict in this case. When the American wants to be alone he goes into a room and shuts the door—he depends on architectural features for screening. For an American to refuse to talk to someone else present in the same room, to give them the "silent treatment," is the ultimate form of rejection and a sure sign of great displeasure. The English, on the other hand, lacking rooms of their own since childhood, never developed the practice of using space as a refuge from others. They have in effect internalized a set of barriers, which they erect and which others are supposed to recognize. Therefore, the more the Englishman shuts himself off when he is with an American the more likely the American is to break in to assure himself that all is well. Tension lasts until the two get to know each other. The important point is that the spatial and architectural needs of each are not the same at all.

Using the Telephone

English internalized privacy mechanisms and the American privacy screen result in very different customs regarding the telephone. There is no wall or door against the telephone. Since it is impossible to tell from the ring who is on the other end of the line, or how urgent his business is, people feel compelled to answer the phone. As one would anticipate, the English when they feel the need to be with their thoughts treat the phone as an intrusion by someone who doesn't know any better. Since it is impossible to tell how preoccupied the other party will be they hesitate to use the phone; instead, they write notes. To phone is to be "pushy" and rude. A letter or telegram may be slower, but it is much less disrupting. Phones are for actual business and emergencies.

I used this system myself for several years when I lived in Santa Fe, New Mexico, during the depression. I dispensed with a phone because it cost money. Besides, I cherished the quiet of my tiny mountainside retreat and didn't want to be disturbed. This idiosyncrasy on my part produced a shocked reaction in others. People really didn't know what to do with me. You could see the consternation on their faces when, in answer to the question, "How do I get in touch with you?" I would reply, "Write me a post card. I come to the post office every day."

Having provided most of our middle-class citizens with private rooms and escape from the city to the suburbs, we have then proceeded to penetrate their most private spaces in their home with a most public device, the telephone. Anyone can reach us at any time. We are, in fact, so available that elaborate devices have to be devised so that busy people can function. The greatest skill and tact must be exercised in the message-screening process so that others will not be offended. So far our technology has not kept up with the needs of people to be alone with either their families or their thoughts. The problem stems from the fact that it is impossible to tell from the phone's ring who is calling and how urgent his business is. Some people have unlisted phones but then that makes it hard on friends who come to town who want to get in touch with them. The government solution is to have special phones for important people (traditionally red). The red line bypasses secretaries, coffee breaks, busy signals, and teen-agers, and is connected to White House, State Department, and Pentagon switchboards.

Neighbors

Americans living in England are remarkably consistent in their reactions to the English. Most of them are hurt and puzzled because they were brought up on American neighboring patterns and don't interpret the English ones correctly. In England propinquity means nothing. The fact that you live next door to a family does not entitle you to visit, borrow from, or socialize with them, or your children to play with theirs. Accurate figures on the number of Americans who adjust well to the English are difficult to obtain. The basic attitude of the English toward the Americans is tinged by our ex-colonial status. This attitude is much more in awareness and therefore more likely to be expressed than the unspoken right of the Englishman to maintain his privacy against the world. To the best of my knowledge, those who have tried to relate to the English purely on the basis of propinquity seldom if ever succeed. They may get to know and even like their neighbors, but it won't be because they live next door, because English relationships are patterned not according to space but according to social status.

Whose Room Is the Bedroom?

In upper middle-class English homes, it is the man, not the woman, who has the privacy of the bedroom, presumably as protection from children who haven't yet internalized the English patterns of privacy. The man, not the woman, has a dressing room; the man also has a study which affords privacy. The Englishman is fastidious about his clothes and expects to spend a great deal of time and attention in their purchase. In contrast, English women approach the buying of clothes in a manner reminiscent of the American male.

Talking Loud and Soft

Proper spacing between people is maintained in many ways. Loudness of the voice is one of the mechanisms which also varies from culture to culture. In England and in Europe generally, Americans are continually accused of loud talking, which is a function of two forms of vocal control: (a) loudness, and (b) modulation for direction. Americans increase the volume as a function of distance, using several levels (whisper, normal voice, loud shout, etc.). In many situations, the more gregarious Americans do not care if they can be overheard. In fact, it is part of their openness showing that we have nothing to hide. The English do care, for to get along without private offices and not intrude they have developed skills in beaming the voice toward the person they are talking to, carefully adjusting it so that it just barely overrides the

PLATES 15 AND 16. Fixed-feature space describes the material objects and internalized design of rooms and buildings that govern human behavior. These two views of an over-crowded, poorly planned kitchen illustrate the frequent lack of congruence in modern building between design elements and the activities to be performed.

PLATE 17. San Marco Square in Venice is widely recognized as an ideal example of the successful enclosure of a large space. The freedom and relaxation these people obviously feel convey the sense of a space that is both exciting and comfortable.

PLATE 18. Sculpture adds a dimension to space, particularly if it can be felt, rubbed, patted, leaned against or climbed upon.

PLATES 19 AND 20. Proxemic patterns are often excellent clues to cultural differences. These two French scenes, showing the crowded spacing of cafe tables and a crowd of persons listening to an outdoor talk, indicate the French tendency to pack together more closely than do northern Europeans, English, and Americans, and suggest the resulting high sensory involvement evident in many aspects of French life.

PLATE 21. Japanese use and arrangement of space is beautifully illustrated by the fifteenth-century Zen monastery garden of Ryoanji outside the old capital of Kyoto. The placement of fifteen rocks rising from a sea of crushed gravel suggests the Japanese employment of all the senses in the perception of space and the tendency to lead the individual to a spot where he can discover something for himself, a tendency reflected in other areas of Japanese life as well.

PLATE 22. The Arabs show a great overt sensitivity to architectural crowding and require enclosed spaces with unobstructed views. The "spite house" in Beirut was built to punish a neighbor by denying him a view of the Mediterranean.

PLATES 23 AND 24. Public housing constructed for low income groups often dresses up and hides but fails to solve many basic human problems. High-rise apartment buildings are less distressing to look at than slums but more disturbing to live in than much of what they replaced.

PLATES 25 AND 26. Two recent residential developments give hope that the gradual strangulation of the hearts of the cities can be reversed.

PLATE 25 *(above)*. In Marina City, Chicago, Bertrand Goldberg has designed circular apartment towers with lower floors that spiral upward and provide open-air, off-street parking facilities for the residents. Complete with marketing and entertainment facilities, the towers offer protection from weather and traffic disturbances.

PLATE 26 *(below)*. Another promising approach to civic design is that developed by Chloethiel Smith, a Washington, D.C., architect. In her southwest Washington apartments, she has managed to create interesting, esthetically satisfying, diverse, and humanly congenial solutions to problems of urban renewal.

background noise and distance. For the English to be overheard is to intrude on others, a failure in manners and a sign of socially inferior behavior. However, because of the way they modulate their voices the English in an American setting may sound and look conspiratorial to Americans, which can result in their being branded as troublemakers.

Eye Behavior

A study of eye behavior reveals some interesting contrasts between the two cultures. Englishmen in this country have trouble not only when they want to be alone and shut themselves off but also when they want to interact. They never know for sure whether an American is listening. We, on the other hand, are equally unsure as to whether the English have understood us. Many of these ambiguities in communication center on differences in the use of the eyes. The Englishman is taught to pay strict attention, to listen carefully, which he must do if he is polite and there are not protective walls to screen out sound. He doesn't bob his head or grunt to let you know he understands. He blinks his eyes to let you know that he has heard you. Americans, on the other hand, are taught not to stare. We look the other person straight in the eye without wavering only when we want to be particularly certain that we are getting through to him.

The gaze of the American directed toward his conversational partner often wanders from one eye to the other and even leaves the face for long periods. Proper English listening behavior includes immobilization of the eyes at social distance, so that whichever eye one looks at gives the appearance of looking straight at you. In order to accomplish this feat, the Englishman must be eight or more feet away. He is too close when the 12-degree horizontal span of the macula won't permit a steady gaze. At less than eight feet, one *must* look at either one eye or the other.

THE FRENCH

The French who live south and east of Paris belong generally to that complex of cultures which border the Mediterranean. Members of this group pack together more closely than do northern Europeans, English, and Americans. Mediterranean use of space can be seen in the crowded trains, buses, automobiles, sidewalk cafés, and in the homes of the people. The exceptions are, of course, in the châteaus and villas of the rich. Crowded living normally means high sensory involvement. Evidence of French emphasis on the senses appears not only in the way the French eat, entertain, talk, write, crowd together in cafés, but can even be seen in the way they make their maps. These maps are extraordinarily well thought out and so designed that the traveler can find the most detailed information. One can tell from using these maps that the French employ all their senses. These maps make it possible for you to get around and they also tell you where you can enjoy a view; where you'll find picturesque drives, and, in some instances, places to rest, refresh yourself, take a walk, and even eat a pleasant meal. They inform the traveler which senses he can expect to use and at what points in his journey.

Home and Family

One possible reason why the French love the outdoors is the rather crowded conditions under which many of them live. The French entertain at restaurants and cafés. The home is for the family and the outdoors for recreation and socializing. Yet all the homes I have visited, as well as everything I have been able to learn about French homes, indicate that they are often quite crowded. The working class and the petite bourgeoisie are particularly crowded, which means that the French are sensually much involved with each other. The layout of their offices, homes, towns, cities, and countryside is such as to keep them involved.

In interpersonal encounters this involvement runs high;

when a Frenchman talks to you, he really looks at you and there is no mistaking this fact. On the streets of Paris he looks at the woman he sees very directly. American women returning to their own country after living in France often go through a period of sensory deprivation. Several have told me that because they have grown accustomed to being looked at, the American habit of *not* looking makes them feel as if they didn't exist.

Not only are the French sensually involved with each other, they have become accustomed to what are to us greatly stepped-up sensory inputs. The French automobile is designed in response to French needs. Its small size used to be attributed to a lower standard of living and higher costs of materials; and while there can be no doubt but that cost is a factor, it would be naïve to assume that it was the major factor. The automobile is just as much an expression of the culture as is the language and, therefore, has its characteristic niche in the cultural biotope. Changes in the car will reflect and be reflected in changes elsewhere. If the French drove American cars, they would be forced to give up many ways of dealing with space which they hold quite dear. The traffic along the Champs-Elysées and around the Arc de Triomphe is a cross between the New Jersey Turnpike on a sunny Sunday afternoon and the Indianapolis Speedway. With American-size autos, it would be mass suicide. Even the occasional "compact" American cars in the stream of Parisian traffic look like sharks among minnows. In the United States, the same cars look normal because everything else is in scale. In the foreign setting where they stand out, Detroit iron can be seen for what it is. The American behemoths give bulk to the ego and prevent overlapping of personal spheres inside the car so that each passenger is only marginally involved with the others. I do not mean by this that all Americans are alike and have been forced into the Detroit mold. But since Detroit won't produce what is wanted, many Americans prefer the smaller, more maneuverable European cars which fit their personalities and needs more closely. Nevertheless, if one simply looks at the styles of the French cars, one sees greater emphasis on individuality than in the United States. Compare the Peugeot, the Citroen, the Renault and the Dauphine and the little 2

C.V. shoebox. It would take years and years of style changes to produce such differences in the United States.

French Use of Open Spaces

Because total space needs must be maintained in balance, the urban French have learned to make the most of the parks and the outdoors. To them, the city is something from which to derive satisfaction and so are the people in it. Reasonably clean air, sidewalks up to seventy feet wide, automobiles that will not dwarf humans as they pass on the boulevards make it possible to have outdoor cafés and open areas where people congregate and enjoy each other. Since the French savor and participate in the city itself—its varied sights, sounds, and smells; its wide sidewalks and avenues and parks—the need for insulating space in the automobile may be somewhat less than it is in the United States where humans are dwarfed by skyscrapers and the products of Detroit, visually assaulted by filth and rubbish, and poisoned by smog and carbon dioxide.

The Star and the Grid

There are two major European systems for patterning space. One of these, "the radiating star" which occurs in France and Spain, is sociopetal. The other, the "grid," originated in Asia Minor, adopted by the Romans and carried to England at the time of Caesar, is sociofugal. The French-Spanish system connects all points and functions. In the French subway system, different lines repeatedly come together at places of interest like the Place de la Concorde, the Opéra, and the Madeleine. The grid system separates activities by stringing them out. Both systems have advantages, but a person familiar with one has difficulty using the other.

For example, a mistake in direction in the radiating center-point system becomes more serious the farther one travels. Any error, therefore, is roughly equivalent to taking off in the wrong direction. In the grid system, baseline errors are of the 90-degree or the 180-degree variety and are usually obvious enough to make themselves felt even by those with a poor sense of direction. If you are traveling in the right direction, even though you are one or two blocks off your course, the error is easily rectified at any time. Nevertheless, there are certain inherent advantages in the center-point system. Once one learns to use it, it is easier for example to locate objects or events in space by naming a point on a line. Thus it is possible, even in strange territory, to tell someone to meet you at the 50 KM mark on National Route 20 south of Paris; that is all the information he needs. In contrast, the grid system of co-ordinates involves at least two lines and a point to locate something in space (often many more lines and points, depending on how many turns one has to make). In the star system, it is also possible to integrate a number of different activities in centers in less space than with the grid system. Thus, residential, shopping, marketing, commercial, and recreation areas can both meet and be reached from central points.

It is incredible how many facets of French life the radiating star pattern touches. It is almost as though the whole culture were set up on a model in which power, influence, and control flowed in and out from a series of interlocking centers. There are sixteen major highways running into Paris, twelve into Caen (near Omaha Beach), twelve into Amiens, eleven for Le Mans, and ten for Rennes. Even the figures don't begin to convey the picture of what this arrangement really means, for France is a series of radiating networks that build up into larger and larger centers. Each small center has its own channel, as it were, to the next higher level. As a general rule, the roads between centers do not go through other towns, because each town is connected to others by its own roads. This is in contrast to the American pattern of stringing small towns out like beads on a necklace along the routes that connect principal centers.

In *The Silent Language* I have described how the man in charge of a French office can often be found in the middle—with his minions placed like satellites on strings radiating outward from him. I once had occasion to deal with such a "central figure" when the French member of a team of scientists under my direction wanted a raise because his desk was in the middle! Even De Gaulle bases his international policy on France's central location. There are those, of course, who will say that the fact that the French school system also follows a highly centralized pattern couldn't possibly have any relationship to the layout of offices, subway systems, road networks, and, in fact, the entire nation, but I could not agree with them. Long experience with different patterns of culture has taught me that the basic threads tend to be woven throughout the entire fabric of a society.

The reason for the review of the three European cultures to which the middle class of the United States is most closely linked (historically and culturally) is as much as anything else a means of providing contrast to highlight some of our own implicit patterns. In this review it was shown that different use of the senses leads to very different needs regarding space no matter on what level one cares to consider it. Everything from an office to a town or city will reflect the sense modalities of its builders and occupants. In considering solutions to problems such as urban renewal and city sinks it is essential to know how the populations involved perceive space and how they use their senses. The next chapter deals with people whose spatial worlds are quite different from our own, and from whom we can learn more about ourselves.

XII

PROXEMICS IN A CROSS-CULTURAL CONTEXT: JAPAN AND THE ARAB WORLD

Proxemic patterns play a role in man comparable to display behavior among lower life forms; that is, they simultaneously consolidate the group and isolate it from others by on the one hand reinforcing intragroup identity and on the other making intergroup communication more difficult. Even though man may be physiologically and genetically one species, the proxemic patterns of the Americans and the Japanese often strike one as being as disparate as the territorial display patterns of the American grouse and the Australian bowerbirds described in Chapter II.

JAPAN

In old Japan, space and social organization were interrelated. The Tokugawa shoguns arranged the daimyo, or nobles, in concentric zones around the capital, Ado (Tokyo). Proximity to the core reflected closeness of relationship and loyalty to the shogun; the most loyal formed an inner protective ring. On the other side of the island, across the mountains and to the north and south, were those who were less trusted or whose loyalty was in question. The concept of the center that can be approached from any direction is a well-developed theme in Japanese culture. This entire plan is characteristically Japanese and those who know them will recognize it as a manifestation of a paradigm that functions in virtually all areas of Japanese life.

As noted earlier, the Japanese name intersections rather than the streets leading into them. In fact, each separate corner of the intersection has a different identification. The route itself from point *A* to point *B* seems almost whimsical to the Westerner and is not stressed as it is with us. Not being in the habit of using fixed routes, the Japanese zero in on their destination when they travel across Tokyo. Taxicab drivers have to ask local directions at police booths, not just because streets are not named but because houses are numbered in the order in which they were built. Neighbors often do not know each other and so cannot give directions. In order to cope with this aspect of Japanese space, the American occupation forces after V-J Day named a few main thoroughfares in Tokyo, putting up street signs in English (Avenues A, B, and C). The Japanese waited politely until the end of the occupation to take the signs down. By then, however, the Japanese were trapped by a foreign cultural innovation. They discovered that it is actually helpful to be able to designate a route that connects two points. It will be interesting to see how persistent this change in Japanese culture will be.

It is possible to see the Japanese pattern that emphasizes centers not only in a variety of other spatial arrangements but, as I hope to demonstrate, even in their conversations. The Japanese fireplace (*hibachi*) and its location carries with it an emotional tone that is as strong, if not stronger, than our concept of the hearth. As an old priest once explained, "To really know the Japanese you have to have spent some cold winter evenings snuggled together around the *hibachi*. Everybody sits together. A common quilt covers not only the *hibachi* but everyone's lap as well. In this way the heat is held in. It's when your hands touch and you feel the warmth of their bodies and everyone feels together—that's when you get to know the Japanese. That is the real Japan!" In psychological terms there is positive reinforcement toward the center of the room and negative reinforcement toward the edges (which is where the cold comes from in the winter). Is it any wonder then that the Japanese have been known to say that our rooms look bare (because the centers are bare).

Another side of the center-edge contrast has to do with how and under what circumstances one moves and what is considered to be fixed-feature and what semifixed-feature space. To us the walls of a house are fixed. In Japan they are semifixed. The walls are movable and rooms are multipurpose. In the Japanese country inns (the *ryokan*), the guest discovers that things come to him while the scene shifts. He sits in the middle of the room on the *tatami* (mat) while sliding panels are opened or closed. Depending on the time of day, the room can include all outdoors or it can be shrunk in stages until all that remains is a boudoir. A wall slides back and a meal is brought in. When the meal is over and it is time to sleep, bedding is unrolled in the same spot in which eating, cooking, thinking, and socializing took place. In the morning, when the room is again opened to all outdoors, bright rays of sunshine or the subtle pine scent of the mountain mists penetrates intimate space and sweeps it refreshingly clean.

A fine example of the differences in the perceptual world of the East and the West is the Japanese film *Woman in the Dunes*. The sensual involvement of the Japanese was never more clearly illustrated than in this film. Viewing it one has the feeling of being inside the skin of the screen subjects. At times it is impossible to identify what part of the body one is looking at. The lens of the camera travels slowly, examining every detail of the body. The landscape of the skin is enlarged; its texture is seen as topography, at least by Western eyes. Goose pimples are large enough to be examined individually while grains of sand become like rough quartz pebbles. The experience is not unlike that of looking at the pulsing life of a fish embryo under a microscope.

One of the terms most frequently used by Americans to describe the Japanese *modus operandi* is the word "indirection." An American banker who had spent years in Japan and made the minimum possible accommodation told me that what he found most frustrating and difficult was their indirection. "An old-style Japanese," he complained, "can drive a man crazy faster than anything I know. They talk around and around and around a point and never do get to it." What he did not realize, of course, was that American insistence on "coming to the point" quickly is just as frustrating to the Japanese, who do not understand why we have to be so "logical" all the time.

Young Jesuit missionaries working in Japan have great difficulty at first, for their training works against them. The syllogism on which they depend to make their points clashes with some of the most basic patterns of Japanese life. Their dilemma is: to be true to their training and fail, or to depart from it and succeed. The most successful Jesuit missionary in Japan at the time of my 1957 visit violated group norms when he espoused local custom. After a brief syllogistic introduction he would switch and talk around the point and dwell at length on what wonderful *feelings* (important to the Japanese) one had if one was a Catholic. What interested me was that even though his Catholic brothers knew what he was doing and could observe his success, the hold of their own culture was sufficiently strong so that few could bring themselves to follow his example and violate their own mores.

How Crowded Is Crowded?

To the Westerner of a non-contact group, "crowding" is a word with distasteful connotations. The Japanese I have known prefer crowding, at least in certain situations. They feel it is congenial to sleep close together on the floor, which they refer to as "Japanese style" as contrasted with "American style." It is not surprising, therefore, to discover that according to Donald Keene, author of *Living Japan,* there is no Japanese word for privacy. Yet one cannot say that the concept of privacy does not exist among the Japanese but only that it is very different from the Western conception. While a Japanese may not want to be alone and doesn't mind having people milling around him, he has strong feelings against sharing a wall of his house or apartment with others. He considers his house and the *zone immediately surrounding it* as one structure. This free area, this sliver of space, is considered to be as much a part of the house as the roof. Traditionally, it contains a garden even though tiny, which gives the householder direct contact with nature.

The Japanese Concept of Space Including the Ma

Differences between the West and Japan are not limited to moving around the point *vs.* coming to the point, or the stressing of lines as contrasted with intersections. The entire experience of space in the most essential respects is different from that of Western culture. When Westerners think and talk about space, they mean the distance between objects. In the West, we are taught to perceive and to react to the arrangements of objects and to think of space as "empty." The meaning of this becomes clear only when it is contrasted with the Japanese, who are trained to give *meaning* to spaces—to perceive the shape and arrangement of spaces; for this they have a word, *ma*. The *ma*, or interval, is a basic building block in all Japanese spatial experience. It is functional not only in flower arrangements but apparently is a hidden consideration in the layout of all other spaces. Japanese skill in the handling and arrangement of the *ma* is extraordinary and produces admiration and occasionally even awe in Europeans. Skill in handling spaces is epitomized in the fifteenth century Zen monastery garden of Ryoanji outside the old capital of Kyoto. The garden itself comes as a surprise.  Walking through the darkened, paneled main building one rounds a bend and is suddenly in the presence of a powerful creative force—fifteen rocks rising from a sea of crushed gravel. Viewing Ryoanji is an emotional experience. One is overcome  by the order, serenity, and the discipline of extreme simplicity. Man and nature are somehow transformed and can be viewed as in harmony. There is also a philosophical message regarding man's relation to nature. The grouping is such that no matter where one sits to contemplate the scene, one of the rocks that make up the garden is always hidden (perhaps another clue to the Japanese mind). They believe that memory and imagination should always participate in perceptions.

Part of the Japanese skill in creating gardens stems from the fact that in the perception of space the Japanese employ vision and all the other senses as well. Olfaction, shifts in temperature, humidity, light, shade, and color are worked together in such a way as to enhance the use of the whole body as a sensing organ. In contrast to the single point perspective of Renaissance and Baroque painters, the Japanese garden is designed to be enjoyed from many points of view. The designer makes the garden visitor stop here and there, perhaps to find his footing on a stone in the middle of a pool so that he looks up at precisely the right moment to catch a glimpse of unsuspected vista. *The study of Japanese spaces illustrates their habit of leading the individual to a spot where he can discover something for himself.*

The Arab patterns which are described below have nothing to do with "leading" people anywhere. In the Arab world one is expected to connect widely separated points on his own, and very quickly too. For this reason the reader has to shift gears mentally when considering the Arabs.

THE ARAB WORLD

In spite of over two thousand years of contact, Westerners and Arabs still do not understand each other. Proxemic research reveals some insights into this difficulty. Americans in the Middle East are immediately struck by two conflicting sensations. In public they are compressed and overwhelmed by smells, crowding, and high noise levels; in Arab homes Americans are apt to rattle around, feeling exposed and often somewhat inadequate because of too much space! (The Arab houses and apartments of the middle and upper classes which Americans stationed abroad commonly occupy are much larger than the dwellings such Americans usually inhabit.) Both the high sensory stimulation which is experienced in public places and the basic insecurity which comes from being in a dwelling that is too large provide Americans with an introduction to the sensory world of the Arab.

Behavior in Public

Pushing and shoving in public places is characteristic of Middle Eastern culture. Yet it is not entirely what Americans think it is (being pushy and rude) but stems from a different set of assumptions concerning not only the relations between people but how one experiences the body as well. Paradoxically, Arabs consider northern Europeans and Americans pushy, too. This was very puzzling to me when I started investigating these two views. How could Americans who stand aside and avoid touching be considered pushy? I used to ask Arabs to explain this paradox. None of my subjects was able to tell me specifically what particulars of American behavior were responsible, yet they all agreed that the impression was widespread among Arabs. After repeated unsuccessful attempts to gain insight into the cognitive world of the Arab on this particular point, I filed it away as a question that only time would answer. When the answer came, it was because of a seemingly inconsequential annoyance.

While waiting for a friend in a Washington, D.C., hotel lobby and wanting to be both visible and alone, I had seated myself in a solitary chair outside the normal stream of traffic. In such a setting most Americans follow a rule, which is all the more binding because we seldom think about it, that can be stated as follows: as soon as a person stops or is seated in a public place, there balloons around him a small sphere of privacy which is considered inviolate. The size of the sphere varies with the degree of crowding, the age, sex, and the importance of the person, as well as the general surroundings. Anyone who enters this zone and stays there is intruding. In fact, a stranger who intrudes, even for a specific purpose, acknowledges the fact that he has intruded by beginning his request with "Pardon me, but can you tell me . . . ?"

To continue, as I waited in the deserted lobby, a stranger walked up to where I was sitting and stood close enough so that not only could I easily touch him but I could even hear him breathing. In addition, the dark mass of his body filled the peripheral field of vision on my left side. If the lobby had been crowded with people, I would have understood his behavior, but in an empty lobby his presence made me exceedingly uncomfortable. Feeling annoyed by this intrusion, I moved my body in such a way as to communicate annoyance. Strangely enough, instead of moving away, my actions seemed only to encourage him, because he moved even closer. In spite of the temptation to escape the annoyance, I put aside thoughts of abandoning my post, thinking, "To hell with it.

Why should I move? I was here first and I'm not going to let this fellow drive me out even if he is a boor." Fortunately, a group of people soon arrived whom my tormentor immediately joined. Their mannerisms explained his behavior, for I knew from both speech and gestures that they were Arabs. I had not been able to make this crucial identification by looking at my subject when he was alone because he wasn't talking and he was wearing American clothes.

In describing the scene later to an Arab colleague, two contrasting patterns emerged. My concept and my feelings about my own circle of privacy in a "public" place immediately struck my Arab friend as strange and puzzling. He said, "After all, it's a public place, isn't it?" Pursuing this line of inquiry, I found that in Arab thought I had no rights whatsoever by virtue of occupying a given spot; neither my place nor my body was inviolate! For the Arab, there is no such thing as an intrusion in public. Public means public. With this insight, a great range of Arab behavior that had been puzzling, annoying, and sometimes even frightening began to make sense. I learned, for example, that if A is standing on a street corner and B wants his spot, B is within his rights if he does what he can to make A uncomfortable enough to move. In Beirut only the hardy sit in the last row in a movie theater, because there are usually standees who want seats and who push and shove and make such a nuisance that most people give up and leave. Seen in this light, the Arab who "intruded" on my space in the hotel lobby had apparently selected it for the very reason I had: it was a good place to watch two doors and the elevator. My show of annoyance, instead of driving him away, had only encouraged him. He thought he was about to get me to move.

Another silent source of friction between Americans and Arabs is in an area that Americans treat very informally—the manners and rights of the road. In general, in the United States we tend to defer to the vehicle that is bigger, more powerful, faster, and heavily laden. While a pedestrian walking along a road may feel annoyed he will not think it unusual to step aside for a fast-moving automobile. He knows that because he is moving he does not have the right to the space around him that he has when he is standing still (as I was in the hotel lobby). It appears that the reverse is true with the Arabs who apparently *take on rights to space as they move.* For someone else to move into a space an Arab is also moving into is a violation of his rights. It is infuriating to an Arab to have someone else cut in front of him on the highway. It is the American's cavalier treatment of moving space that makes the Arab call him aggressive and pushy.

Concepts of Privacy

The experience described above and many others suggested to me that Arabs might actually have a wholly contrasting set of assumptions concerning the body and the rights associated with it. Certainly the Arab tendency to shove and push each other in public and to feel and pinch women in public conveyances would not be tolerated by Westerners. It appeared to me that they must not have any concept of a private zone outside the body. This proved to be precisely the case.

In the Western world, the person is synonymous with an individual inside a skin. And in northern Europe generally, the skin and even the clothes may be inviolate. You need permission to touch either if you are a stranger. This rule applies in some parts of France, where the mere touching of another person during an argument used to be legally defined as assault. For the Arab the location of the person in relation to the body is quite different. The person exists somewhere down inside the body. The ego is not completely hidden, however, because it can be reached very easily with an insult. It is protected from touch but not from words. The dissociation of the body and the ego may explain why the public amputation of a thief's hand is tolerated as standard punishment in Saudi Arabia. It also sheds light on why an Arab employer living in a modern apartment can provide his servant with a room that is a boxlike cubicle approximately 5 by 10 by 4 feet in size that is not only hung from the ceiling to conserve floor space but has an opening so that the servant can be spied on.

As one might suspect, deep orientations toward the self such as the one just described are also reflected in the language. This was brought to my attention one afternoon when an Arab colleague who is the author of an Arab-English dictionary arrived in my office and threw himself into a chair in a state of obvious exhaustion. When I asked him what had been going on, he said: "I have spent the entire afternoon trying to find the Arab equivalent of the English word 'rape.' There is no such word in Arabic. All my sources, both written and spoken, can come up with no more than an approximation, such as 'He took her against her will.' There is nothing in Arabic approaching your meaning as it is expressed in that one word."

Differing concepts of the placement of the ego in relation to the body are not easily grasped. Once an idea like this is accepted, however, it is possible to understand many other facets of Arab life that would otherwise be difficult to explain. One of these is the high population density of Arab cities like Cairo, Beirut, and Damascus. According to the animal studies described in the earlier chapters, the Arabs should be living in a perpetual behavioral sink. While it is probable that Arabs are suffering from population pressures, it is also just as possible that continued pressure from the desert has resulted in a cultural adaptation to high density which takes the form described above. Tucking the ego down inside the body shell not only would permit higher population densities but would explain why it is that Arab communications are stepped up as much as they are when compared to northern European communication patterns. Not only is the sheer noise level much higher, but the piercing look of the eyes, the touch of the hands, and the mutual bathing in the warm moist breath during conversation represent stepped-up sensory inputs to a level which many Europeans find unbearably intense.

The Arab dream is for lots of space in the home, which unfortunately many Arabs cannot afford. Yet when he has space, it is very different from what one finds in most American homes. Arab spaces inside their upper middle-class homes are tremendous by our standards. They avoid partitions because Arabs *do not like to be alone.* The form of the home is such as to hold the family together inside a single protective shell, because Arabs are deeply involved with each other. Their personalities are intermingled and take nourishment from each other like the roots and soil. If one is not with people and actively involved in some way, one is deprived of life. An old Arab saying reflects this value: "Paradise without people should not be entered because it is Hell." Therefore, Arabs in the United States often feel socially and sensorially deprived and long to be back where there is human warmth and contact.

Since there is no physical privacy as we know it in the Arab family, not even a word for privacy, one could expect that the Arabs might use some other means to be alone. Their way to be alone is to stop talking. Like the English, an Arab who shuts himself off in this way is not indicating that anything is wrong or that he is withdrawing, only that he wants to be alone with his own thoughts or does not want to be intruded upon. One subject said that her father would come and go for days at a time without saying a word, and no one in the family thought anything of it. Yet for this very reason, an Arab exchange student visiting a Kansas farm failed to pick up the cue that his American hosts were mad at him when they gave him the "silent treatment." He only discovered something was wrong when they took him to town and tried forcibly to put him on a bus to Washington, D.C., the headquarters of the exchange program responsible for his presence in the U.S.

Arab Personal Distances

Like everyone else in the world, Arabs are unable to formulate specific rules for their informal behavior patterns. In fact, they often deny that there are any rules, and they are made anxious by suggestions that such is the case. Therefore, in order to determine how the Arab sets distances, I investigated the use of each sense separately. Gradually, definite and distinctive behavioral patterns began to emerge.

Olfaction occupies a prominent place in the Arab life. Not only is it one of the distance-setting mechanisms, but it is a vital part of a complex system of behavior. Arabs consistently breathe on people when they talk. However, this habit is more than a matter of different manners. To the Arab good smells are pleasing and a way of being involved with each other. To smell one's friend is not only nice but desirable, for to deny him your breath is to act ashamed. Americans, on the other hand, trained as they are not to breathe in people's faces, automatically communicate shame in trying to be polite. Who would expect that when our highest diplomats are putting on their best manners they are also communicating shame? Yet this is what occurs constantly, because diplomacy is not only "eyeball to eyeball" but breath to breath.

By stressing olfaction, Arabs do not try to eliminate all the body's odors, only to enhance them and use them in building human relationships. Nor are they self-conscious about telling others when they don't like the way they smell. A man leaving his house in the morning may be told by his uncle, "Habib, your stomach is sour and your breath doesn't smell too good. Better not talk too close to people today." Smell is even considered in the choice of a mate. When couples are being matched for marriage, the man's go-between will sometimes ask to smell the girl, who may be turned down if she doesn't "smell nice." Arabs recognize that smell and disposition may be linked.

In a word, the olfactory boundary performs two roles in Arab life. It enfolds those who want to relate and separates those who don't. The Arab finds it essential to stay inside the olfactory zone as a means of keeping tab on changes in emotion. What is more, he may feel crowded as soon as he smells something unpleasant. While not much is known about "olfactory crowding," this may prove to be as significant as any other variable in the crowding complex because it is tied directly to the body chemistry and hence to the state of health and emotions. (The reader will remember that it was olfaction in the Bruce effect that suppressed pregnancies in mice.) It is not surprising, therefore, that the olfactory boundary constitutes for the Arabs an informal distance-setting mechanism in contrast to the visual mechanisms of the Westerner.

Facing and Not Facing

One of my earliest discoveries in the field of intercultural communication was that the position of the bodies of people in conversation varies with the culture. Even so, it used to puzzle me that a special Arab friend seemed unable to walk and talk at the same time. After years in the United States, he could not bring himself to stroll along, facing forward while talking. Our progress would be arrested while he edged ahead, cutting slightly in front of me and turning sideways so we could see each other. Once in this position, he would stop. His behavior was explained when I learned that for the Arabs to view the other person peripherally is regarded as impolite, and to sit or stand back-to-back is considered very rude. You must be involved when interacting with Arabs who are friends.

One mistaken American notion is that Arabs conduct all conversations at close distances. This is not the case at all. On social occasions, they may sit on opposite sides of the room and talk across the room to each other. They are, however, apt to take offense when Americans use what are to them ambiguous distances, such as the four- to seven-foot social-consultative distance. They frequently complain that Americans are cold or aloof or "don't care." This was what an elderly Arab diplomat in an American hospital thought when the American nurses used "professional" distance. He had the feeling that he was being ignored, that they might not take good care of him. Another Arab subject remarked, referring to American behavior, "What's the matter? Do I smell bad? Or are they afraid of me?"

Arabs who interact with Americans report experiencing a certain flatness traceable in part to a very different use of the eyes in private and in public as well as between friends and strangers. Even though it is rude for a guest to walk around the Arab home eying things, Arabs look at each other in ways which seem hostile or challenging to the American. One Arab informant said that he was in constant hot water with Americans because of the way he looked at them without the slightest intention of offending. In fact, he had on several occasions barely avoided fights with American men who apparently thought their masculinity was being challenged because of the way he was looking at them. As noted earlier, Arabs look each other in the eye when talking with an intensity that makes most Americans highly uncomfortable.

Involvement

As the reader must gather by now, Arabs are involved with each other on many different levels simultaneously. Privacy in a public place is foreign to them. Business transactions in the bazaar, for example, are not just between buyer and seller, but are participated in by everyone. Anyone who is standing around may join in. If a grownup sees a boy breaking a window, he must stop him even if he doesn't know him. Involvement and participation are expressed in other ways as well. If two men are fighting, the crowd must intervene. On the political level, *to fail to intervene* when trouble is brewing is to take sides, which is what our State Department always seems to be doing. Given the fact that few people in the world today are even remotely aware of the cultural mold that forms their thoughts, it is normal for Arabs to view *our* behavior as though it stemmed from *their* own hidden set of assumptions.

Feelings about Enclosed Spaces

In the course of my interviews with Arabs the term "tomb" kept cropping up in conjunction wtih enclosed space. In a word, Arabs don't mind being crowded by people but hate to be hemmed in by walls. They show a much greater overt sensitivity to architectural crowding than we do. Enclosed space must meet at least three requirements that I know of if it is to satisfy the Arabs: there must be plenty of unobstructed space in which to move around (possibly as much as a thousand square feet); very high ceilings—so high in fact that they do not normally impinge on the visual field; and, in addition, there must be an unobstructed view. It was spaces such as these in which the Americans referred to earlier felt so uncomfortable. One sees the Arab's need for a view expressed in many ways, even negatively, for to cut off a neighbor's view is one of the most effective ways of spiting him. In Beirut one can see what is known locally as the "spite house." It is nothing more than a thick, four-story wall, built at the end of a long fight between neighbors, on a narrow strip of land for the express purpose of denying a view of the Mediterranean to any house built on the land behind. According to one of my informants, there is also a house on a small plot of land between Beirut and Damascus which is completely surrounded by a neighbor's wall built high enough to cut off the view from all windows!

Boundaries

Proxemic patterns tell us other things about Arab culture. For example, the whole concept of the boundary as an abstraction is almost impossible to pin down. In one sense, there are no boundaries. "Edges" of towns, yes, but permanent boundaries out in the country (hidden lines), no. In the course of my work with Arab subjects I had a difficult time translating our concept of a boundary into terms which could be equated with theirs. In order to clarify the distinctions between the two very different definitions, I thought it might be helpful to pinpoint acts which constituted trespass. To date, I have been unable to discover anything even remotely resembling our own legal concept of trespass.

Arab behavior in regard to their own real estate is apparently an extension of, and therefore consistent with, their approach to the body. My subjects simply failed to respond whenever trespass was mentioned. They didn't seem to understand what I meant by this term. This may be explained by the fact that they organize relationships with each other according to closed social systems rather than spatially. For thousands of years Moslems, Marinites, Druses, and Jews have lived in their own villages, each with strong kin affiliations. Their hierarchy of loyalties is: first to one's self, then to kinsman, townsman, or tribesman, co-religionist and/or countryman. Anyone not in these categories is a stranger. Strangers and enemies are very closely linked, if not synonymous, in Arab thought. Trespass in this context is a matter of who you are, rather than a piece of land or a space with a boundary that can be denied to anyone and everyone, friend and foe alike.

In summary, proxemic patterns differ. By examining them it is possible to reveal hidden cultural frames that determine the structure of a given people's perceptual world. Perceiving the world differently leads to differential definitions of what constitutes crowded living, different interpersonal relations, and a different approach to both local and international politics. There are in addition wide discrepancies in the degree to which culture structures involvement, which means that planners should begin to think in terms of different kinds of cities, cities which are consistent with the proxemic patterns of the peoples who live in them. Therefore, it is to a consideration of urban life that I wish to turn in the remaining chapters of this book.

XIII

CITIES AND CULTURE

The implosion of the world population into cities everywhere is creating a series of destructive behavioral sinks more lethal than the hydrogen bomb. Man is faced with a chain reaction and practically no knowledge of the structure of the cultural atoms producing it. If what is known about animals when they are crowded or moved to an unfamiliar biotope is at all relevant to mankind, we are now facing some terrible consequences in our urban sinks. Studies of ethology and comparative proxemics should alert us to the dangers ahead as our rural populations pour into urban centers. The adjustment of these people is not just economic but involves an *entire way of life*. There are the added complexities of dealing with strange communication systems, uncongenial spaces, and the pathology associated with an active, swelling behavioral sink.

The lower-class Negro in the United States poses very special problems in his adjustment to city living, which if they are not solved may well destroy us by making our cities uninhabitable. An often overlooked fact is that lower-class Negroes and middle-class whites are culturally distinct from each other. In many respects, the situation of the American Negro parallels that of the American Indian. The differences between these minority groups and the dominant culture are basic and have to do with such core values as the use and structuring of space, time, and materials, all of which are learned early in life. Some Negro spokesmen have gone so far as to say that no white man could possibly understand the Negro. They are right if they are referring to lower-class Negro culture. However, few people grasp the fact that cultural differences of the type that many Negroes experience as isolating, while exacerbated by prejudice, are not the same as prejudice, nor are they inherently prejudicial. They lie at the core of the human situation and they are as old as man.

A point I want to emphasize is that in the major cities of the United States, people of very different cultures are now in contact with each other in dangerously high concentrations, a situation which brings to mind a study by pathologist Charles Southwick. Southwick discovered that peromyscus mice could tolerate high cage densities until strange mice were introduced. When this occurred there was not only a significant increase in fighting but an increase in the weight of the adrenal glands as well as the blood eosimphil count (both of which are associated with stress). Now even if it were possible to abolish all prejudice and discrimination and erase a disgraceful past, the lower-class Negro in American cities would still be confronted with a syndrome that is currently extremely stressful: the sink (popularly referred to as "the jungle"), the existence of great cultural differences between himself and the dominant white middle class of America, and a completely foreign biotope.

Sociologists Glazer and Moynihan in their fascinating book, *Beyond the Melting Pot,* have clearly demonstrated that in fact there is no melting pot in American cities. Their study focused on New York but their conclusions could apply to many other cities. The major ethnic groups of American cities maintain distinct identities for several generations. Yet our housing and city planning programs seldom take these ethnic differences into account. Even while writing this chapter I was asked to consult with an urban planning agency which was considering the problem of urban life in 1980. The entire plan under discussion was predicated on complete absences of both ethnic and class differences by this date. Nothing in man's past indicates to me that these differences will disappear in one generation!

THE NEED FOR CONTROLS

Lewis Mumford states that the primary reason for Hammurabi's code was to combat the lawlessness of the people flocking into the early Mesopotamian cities. Since then a lesson repeatedly brought home about the relationship of man to the city is the need for enforced laws to replace tribal custom. Laws and law enforcement agencies are present in cities all over the world, but at times they find it difficult to cope with the problems facing them and they need help. An aid to law and order that has not been used to the fullest extent possible is the power of custom and public opinion in the ethnic enclaves. These enclaves perform many useful purposes; one of the most important is that they act as lifetime reception areas in which the second generation can learn to make the transition to city life. The principal problem with the enclave as it is now placed in the city is that its size is limited. When membership increases at a rate greater than the capacity to turn rural peoples into city dwellers (which is the number that moves out of the enclave), only two choices remain: territorial growth or overcrowding.

If the enclave cannot expand and fails to maintain a healthy density (which varies with each ethnic group), a sink develops. The normal capacities of law enforcement agencies are not able to deal with sinks. This is illustrated by what has happened in New York City with its Puerto Rican and Negro populations. According to a recent *Time* report, 232,000 people are packed into three and a half square miles in Harlem. Apart from letting the sink run its course and destroy the city, there is an alternative solution: *introduce design features that will counteract the ill effects of the sink but not destroy the enclave in the process.* In animal populations, the solution is simple enough and frighteningly like what we see in our urban renewal programs as well as our suburban sprawl. To increase density in a rat population and maintain healthy specimens, put them in boxes so they can't see each other, clean their cages, and give them enough to eat. You can pile the boxes up as many stories as you wish. Unfortunately, caged animals become stupid, which is a very heavy price to pay for a super filing system! The question we must ask ourselves is, How far can we afford to travel down the road of sensory deprivation in order to file people away? One of man's most critical needs, therefore, is for principles for designing spaces that will maintain a healthy density, a healthy interaction rate, a proper amount of involvement, and a continuing sense of ethnic identification. The creation of such principles will require the combined efforts of many diverse specialists all working closely together on a massive scale.

This point was stressed in 1964 at the second Delos conference. Organized by the Greek architect, town planner, and builder C. A. Doxiadis, the Delos conferences annually assemble an impressive array of experts from all over the world whose knowledge and skills can contribute to the proper study of what Doxiadis has termed ekistics (the study of settlements). The conclusions reached by this group were: (1) Both the New Town programs in England and Israel are based on inadequate, century-old data. For one thing, the towns were too small, yet even the greater size now proposed by English planners is based on very limited research. (2) Although the public is aware of the desperate situation of the ever-growing megalopolis, nothing is being done about it. (3) The combination of the catastrophic growth of both the number of automobiles and the population is creating a chaotic situation in which there are no self-correcting features. Either automobiles are precipitated to the heart of the city by freeways (leading to the choked-up effect present in London and New York City) or the town gives way to the automobile, disappearing under a maze of freeways, as is the case with Los Angeles. (4) To keep our economies growing, few activities would promote such a wide spectrum of industries, services, and skills as rebuilding the cities of the world. (5) Planning, education, and research in ekistics must be not only co-ordinated and underwritten but raised to the highest level of priority in governments.

PSYCHOLOGY AND ARCHITECTURE

To solve formidable urban problems, there is the need not only for the usual coterie of experts—city planners, architects, engineers of all types, economists, law enforcement specialists, traffic and transportation experts, educators, lawyers, social workers, and political scientists—but for a number of new experts. Psychologists, anthropologists, and ethologists are seldom, if ever, prominently featured as permanent members of city planning departments but they should be. Research budgets must not be whimsically turned on and off as has happened in the past. When good, workable plans are developed, planners must not be forced to witness a breakdown in implementation which is so often excused on the grounds of politics or expediency. Also, planning and renewal must not be separated; instead, renewal must be an integral part of planning.

Consider the public housing constructed for low income groups in Chicago which has tended to dress up and hide but not solve the basic problem. Bear in mind that the low income population which is pouring into Chicago and many other American cities is largely Negro and comes from rural areas or small towns in the South. Most of these people have had no tradition or experience in urban living. Like the Puerto Ricans and Appalachian whites, many of the Negroes also suffer from a totally inadequate education. Row after row of high-rise apartments is less distressing to look at than slums but more disturbing to live in than much of what it replaced. The Negroes have been particularly outspoken in their condemnation of high-rise housing. All they see in it is white domination, a monument to a failure in ethnic relations. They joke about how the white man is now piling Negro on top of Negro, stacking them up in high rises. The high rise fails to solve many basic human problems. As one tenant described his building to me: "It's no place to raise a family. A mother can't look out for her kids if they are fifteen floors down in the playground. They get beaten up by the rough ones, the elevators are unsafe and full of filth (people in defiance against the buildings use them as toilets), they are slow and break down. When I want to go home I think twice because it may take me half an hour to get the elevator. Did you ever have to walk up fifteen floors when the elevator was broken? You don't do *that* too often. . . ."

Happily, some architects are beginning to think in terms of two-, three-, and four-story developments designed with a view to human safety. There is very little data, however, on what kind of spaces are best suited to the Negro. My own experience dates back to World War II when I served with a Negro engineer general services regiment. The regiment assembled in Texas, and participated in all five European campaigns. However, it wasn't until we reached the Philippines that the men found a life on a *scale* that suited them. They could easily see themselves adapting to the Philippine society and economy where a man could set himself up in business in a bamboo stall no bigger than two telephone booths. The open market place with all its activity seems more suitable to the proxemic needs of the Negro than crowded American stores which are enclosed by walls and windows.

In other words, I think that it will ultimately be proved that *scale* is a key factor in planning towns, neighborhoods, and housing developments. Most important, urban scale must be consistent with ethnic scale, since each ethnic group seems to have developed its own scale.

There are in addition class differences, which are reported in the work of psychologist Marc Fried and sociologists Herbert Gans, Peggy Gleicher, and Chester Hartman, in a series of important publications on Boston's West End.

The Boston plans for slum clearance and urban renewal failed to take into account the fact that the working-class neighborhoods were quite different from those of the middle class. The West End residents were highly involved with each other; to them the hallways, the stores, the churches, and even the streets provided an essential part of living together in a community. As Hartman points out, in computing population density in the West End there was actually several times the living space available than would be apparent if judged by middle-class standards based solely on the dwelling unit. An additional point was made about the "urban village"

(Gans's term). The Boston West End was a device for turning immigrant villagers into city dwellers, a process which required about three generations. If it had to be "renewed" a more satisfactory solution would have been renovation rather than destruction of the entire neighborhood, which encompassed not only buildings but social systems as well. For when urban renewal forced removal to more modern but less integrated spaces, a significant number of Italians became depressed and apparently lost much of their interest in life. Their world had been shattered, not through malice or design but with the best of intentions, because in Fried's words: "'. . . home' is not merely an apartment or a house but a local area in which some of the most meaningful aspects of life are experienced." The relationship of the West Enders to their urban village was in addition to everything else a matter of scale. The "street" was both familiar and intimate.

While very little is known about something as abstract as scale, I am convinced that it represents a facet of the human requirement that man is ultimately going to have to understand, for it directly affects the judgment of what constitutes proper population density. In addition, setting standards for healthy urban densities is doubly difficult because the basic rules for estimating the proper size of the family dwelling unit are unknown. In the last few years the sizes of dwelling spaces have had a way of slipping unnoticed from barely adequate to completely inadequate as economic and other pressures increase. Not just the poor but even the well-to-do find themselves squeezed by high-rise speculative builders who shave six inches here and a foot there to lower costs and increase profits. Nor can individual units be considered out of context. An apartment which is barely adequate becomes uninhabitable to some people at the exact moment that a rising apartment house next door cuts off the view.

PATHOLOGY AND OVERCROWDING

Like the link between cancer and smoking, the cumulative effects of crowding are usually not experienced until the damage has been done. So far, most of what is known of the human side of cities are the bare facts of crime, illegitimacy, inadequate education, and illness; our most crying need at present is for imaginative research on a massive scale. Although there are many studies of urban life that will prove to be relevant once the relationship of the urban sink to human pathology has been accepted, I know only one which relates directly to the consequences of insufficient space. This research was done by the Chombart de Lauwes, a French husband-and-wife team who combine the skills of sociology and psychology. They produced some of the first statistical data on the consequences of crowding in urban housing. With typical French thoroughness the Chombart de Lauwes collected measurable data on every conceivable aspect of the family life of the French worker. At first they recorded and computed crowding in terms of the number of residents per dwelling unit. This index revealed very little and the Chombart de Lauwes then decided to use a new index to establish crowding—*the number of square meters per person per unit*. The results of this index were startling; when the space available was below eight to ten square meters per person social and physical pathologies doubled! Illness, crime, and crowding were definitely linked. When the space available rose *above* fourteen square meters per person, the incidence of pathology of both types also increased, but not so sharply. The Chombart de Lauwes were at a loss to explain the latter figure except to say that families in the second category were usually upwardly mobile and tended to devote more attention to getting ahead than they did to their children. A note of caution must be introduced here. There is nothing magic about ten to thirteen square meters of space. This figure is only applicable to a very limited segment of the French population at a particular time and has no demonstrable relevance to any other population. To compute crowding for different ethnic groups it is necessary to recall for a moment the earlier chapters dealing with the senses.

The degree to which peoples are sensorially involved with each other, and how they use time, determine not only at what point they are crowded but the methods for relieving crowding as well. Puerto Ricans and Negroes have a much higher involvement ratio than New Englanders and Americans of German or Scandinavian stock. Highly involved people apparently require higher densities than less involved people, and they may also require more protection or screening from outsiders. It is absolutely essential that we learn more about how to compute the maximum, minimum, and optimum density of the different cultural enclaves that make up our cities.

MONOCHRONIC AND POLYCHRONIC TIME

Time and the way it is handled have a lot to do with the structuring of space. In *The Silent Language,* I described two contrasting ways of handling time, monochronic and polychronic. Monochronic is characteristic of low-involvement peoples, who compartmentalize time; they schedule one thing at a time and become disoriented if they have to deal with too many things at once. Polychronic people, possibly because they are so much involved with each other, tend to keep several operations going at once, like jugglers. Therefore, the monochronic person often finds it easier to function if he can separate activities in space, whereas the polychronic person tends to collect activities. If, however, these two types are interacting with each other, much of the difficulty they experience can be overcome by the proper structuring of space. Monochronic northern Europeans, for example, find the constant interruptions of polychronic southern Europeans almost unbearable because it seems that nothing ever gets done. Since order is *not* important to the southern Europeans the customer with the most "push" gets served first even though he may have been the last to enter.

To reduce the polychronic effect, one must reduce involvement, which means separating activities with as much screening as necessary. The other side of the coin is that monochronic people serving polychronic customers must reduce or eliminate physical screening so that people can establish contact. This often means physical contact. For the businessman who serves Latin Americans the success of the settee as contrasted with the desk is an example of what I mean. We have yet to apply even simple principles such as these to the planning of urban spaces. The highly involved polychronic Neapolitan builds and uses the Galeria Umberto where everyone can get together. The Spanish plaza and the Italian piazza serve both involvement and polychronic functions, whereas the strung-out Main Street so characteristic of the United States reflects not only our structuring of time but our lack of involvement in others. Inasmuch as our large cities now incorporate significant elements of both of the types represented above, it might have a salutary effect on the relationships between the two groups if both types of spaces were provided.

City planners should go even further in creating congenial spaces that will encourage and strengthen the cultural enclave. This will serve two purposes: first, it will assist the city and the enclave in the transformation process that takes place generation by generation as country folk are converted to city dwellers; and second, it will strengthen social controls that combat lawlessness. As it is now, we have built lawlessness into our enclaves by letting them turn into sinks. In the words of Barbara Ward, we have to find some way of making the "ghetto" respectable. This means not only that they will be safe but that people can move on when the enclave has performed its functions.

In the course of planning our new cities and revamping our old ones, we might consider positively reinforcing man's continuing need to belong to a social group akin to the old neighborhood where he is known, has a place, and where people have a sense of responsibility for each other. Apart from the ethnic enclave, virtually everything about American cities today is sociofugal and drives men apart, alienating them from each other. The recent and shocking instances in which people have been beaten and even murdered while their "neighbors" looked on without even picking up a phone indicates how far this trend toward alienation has progressed.

THE AUTOMOBILE SYNDROME

How did we reach this state of affairs? One knows intuitively that there are many explanations in addition to the design and layout of buildings and spaces. There is, however, a technical artifact built into our culture which has completely altered our way of life upon which we are now so completely dependent on to satisfy so many needs that it is difficult to conceive of our ever giving it up. I am referring, of course, to the automobile. The automobile is the greatest consumer of public and personal space yet created by man. In Los Angeles, the automobile town par excellence, Barbara Ward found that 60 to 70 per cent of the space is devoted to cars (streets, parking, and freeways). The car gobbles up spaces in which people might meet. Parks, sidewalks, everything goes to the automobile.

There are additional consequences of this syndrome that are worth considering. Not only do people no longer wish to walk, but it is not possible for those who do wish to, to find a *place* to walk. This not only makes people flabby but cuts them off from each other. When people walk, they get to know each other if only by sight. With automobiles the opposite is true. The dirt, noise, exhaust, parked cars, and smog have made the urban outdoors too unpleasant. In addition, most experts agree that the flabby muscles and reduced circulation of the blood that come from lack of regular exercise make man much more prone to heart attacks.

Yet there is no inherent incompatibility between man in an urban setting and the automobile. It's all a matter of proper planning and built-in design features which separate cars from people, a point stressed by the architect Victor Gruen in *The Heart of Our Cities*. There are already numerous examples of how this can be done by imaginative planning.

Paris is known as a city in which the outdoors has been made attractive to people and where it is not only possible but pleasurable to stretch one's legs, breathe, sniff the air, and "take in" the people and the city. The sidewalks along the Champs-Elysées engender a wonderful expansive feeling associated with a hundred-foot separation of one's self from the traffic. It is noteworthy that the little streets and alleys too narrow to accept most vehicles not only provide variety but are a constant reminder that Paris is for *people*. Venice is without a doubt one of the most wonderfully satisfying cities in the world, with an almost universal appeal. The most striking features of Venice are the absence of vehicular traffic, the variety of spaces, and the wonderful shops. San Marco Square with automobiles parked in the middle would be a disaster and totally unthinkable!

Florence, while different from Paris or Venice, is a stimulating city for the pedestrian. The sidewalks in the central portion of town are narrow so that walking from the Ponte Vecchio to Piazza della Signoria one meets people face to face and has to step aside or go around them. The automobile does not fit in with the design of Florence and if the townspeople were to ban vehicular traffic from the center of town, the transformation could be extraordinary.

The automobile not only seals its occupants in a metal and glass cocoon, cutting them off from the outside world, but it has a way of actually decreasing the sense of movement through space. Loss of the sense of movement comes not only from insulation from road surfaces and noise but is visual as well. The driver on the freeway moves *in a stream of traffic* while visual detail at close distances is blurred by speed.

Man's entire organism was designed to move through the environment at less than five miles per hour. How many can remember what it is like to be able to see everything nearby quite sharply as one walks through the countryside for a week, a fortnight, or a month? At walking speeds even the nearsighted can see trees, shrubbery, leaves and grass, the surfaces of rocks and stones, grains of sand, ants, beetles, caterpillars, even gnats, flies and mosquitoes, to say nothing of birds and other wildlife. Not only is near vision blurred by the speed of the automobile but one's relationship to the countryside is vastly altered. I realized this once while riding my horse from Santa Fe, New Mexico, to the Indian reservations in northern Arizona. My route took me north of Mt. Taylor, which I knew well because I had passed its southern edge fifty times on the highway from Albuquerque to Gallup. Driving west at automobile speeds one watches the mountain rotate as different faces are presented. The whole panorama is finished in one or two hours and ends with the red-walled Navajo sandstone cliffs outside of Gallup. At walking speed (which is all one can do on a horse if great distances are to be covered) the mountain does not appear to move or rotate. Space and distance and the land itself have more meaning.

As speed increases, sensory involvement falls off until one is experiencing real sensory deprivation. In modern American cars the kinesthetic sense of space is absent. Kinesthetic space and visual space are insulated from each other and are no longer mutually reinforcing. Soft springs, soft cushions, soft tires, power steering, and monotonously smooth pavements create an unreal experience of the earth. One manufacturer has even gone so far as to advertise his product by showing a car full of happy people *floating on a cloud above the road!*

Automobiles insulate man not only from the environment but from human contact as well. They permit only the most limited types of interaction, usually competitive, aggressive, and destructive. If people are to be brought together again, given a chance to get acquainted with each other and involved in nature, some fundamental solutions must be found to the problems posed by the automobile.

CONTAINED COMMUNITY BUILDINGS

Many factors in addition to the automobile are combining to gradually strangle the hearts of our cities. It is not possible to say at this time whether the flight of the middle class from the city can be reversed, or what the ultimate consequences will be if this trend is not reversed. There are, however, a few small encouraging spots on the horizon well worth watching. One of them is Marina City, Bertrand Goldberg's circular apartment towers in Chicago. The towers occupy a city block downtown on the edge of the Chicago River. The lower floors spiral upward and provide open-air, off-street parking facilities for the apartment residents. Marina City has many other features that answer the needs of city dwellers: restaurants, bars and taverns, a super market, liquor store, theater, ice skating rink, a bank, boat basins, and even an art gallery. It is safe, protected from weather and possible city violence (you don't need to go outside for anything). If tenant turnover isn't too great because of the small spaces in the apartments, some tenants may actually get to know each other and develop a sense of community. The view of a city, especially at night, is a delight and one of its greatest assets, yet how few people get to appreciate it? Visually, the design of Marina City is superb. Viewed from a distance, the towers are like the pine trees on the ridges around San Francisco Bay; the balconies stimulate the fovea and beckon the viewer to come closer, promising new surprises with each shift in the visual field. Another promising approach to civic design is that developed by Chloethiel Smith, an architect in Washington, D.C. Miss Smith, always concerned with the human side of architecture, has managed to create interesting, esthetically satisfying, and humanly congenial solutions to problems in urban renewal. Automobiles are handled as inconspicuously as possible and kept away from people.

City planners and architects should welcome opportunities to experiment with radically new, integrated forms that will hold an entire community. One of the advantages of Marina City, apart from the excitement it generates visually, is that it represents a definite, well-delineated amount of contained space without the killing effect of long corridors. There will be no spilling out or spreading or sprawling from this structure. Its principal defect is the cramped living space, which a number of the tenants I have talked to experience as unduly confining. In the heart of the city one needs more space in the home, not less. The home must be an antidote for city stresses.

As now constituted, the American city is extraordinarily wasteful, emptying itself each night and every weekend. One would think that efficiency-minded Americans could do better. The result of the suburbanization of our cities is that the remaining residents are now predominantly the overcrowded impoverished and the very rich, with a sprinkling of holdouts from the middle class. As a result, the city is very unstable.

PROSPECTUS FOR CITY PLANNING OF THE FUTURE

The city has existed in various forms for some five thousand years and it seems unlikely that there will be a ready-made substitute for it. There is no doubt in my mind that the city is in addition to everything else an expression of the culture of the people who produced it, an extension of society that performs many complex, interrelated functions, some of which we are not even aware of. From the perspective of the anthropologist one approaches the city with some degree of awe and the knowledge that we do not know nearly enough to plan intelligently for the city of the future. Yet plan we must because the future has caught up with us. There are several points which are crucial to the solutions of the numerous problems facing us today. They are:

1. Finding suitable methods for computing and measuring human scale in all its dimensions including the hidden dimensions of culture. The proper meshing of human scale and the scale imposed by the automobile presents us with a great challenge.

2. Making constructive use of the ethnic enclave. Somehow there is a close identification between the image that man has of himself and the space that he inhabits. Much of today's popular literature devoted to the search for identity reflects this relationship. A very real effort should be made to discover and satisfy the needs of the Spanish American, the Negro, and other ethnic groups so that the spaces which they inhabit are not only compatible with their needs but reinforce the positive elements of their culture that help to provide identity and strength.

3. Conserving large, readily available outdoor spaces. London, Paris, and Stockholm are models which if properly adapted could prove useful for American city planners. The great danger in the United States today is the continuing destruction of the outdoors. This can prove extraordinarily serious, if not fatal, to the entire country. Solving the problem of the outdoors and man's need for contact with nature is complicated by the increasing incidence of crime and violence associated with our city sinks. Parks and beaches are daily becoming more dangerous. This only intensifies the sense of crowding which urban residents experience when they are cut off from recreational facilities. In addition to city recreation areas and green belts, setting aside large sections of primitive outdoors is one of our greatest needs. Failure to take this step now could mean catastrophe for future generations.

4. Preserving useful, satisfying old buildings and neighbor-

hoods from "the bomb" of urban renewal. Not all new things are necessarily good nor are all old things bad. There are many places in our cities—sometimes only a few houses or a cluster of houses—which deserve to be preserved. They afford continuity with the past and they lend variety to our townscapes.

In this brief review I have said nothing about the very great strides the English have made in urban renewal under the London Plan, first set forth by Sir Patrick Abercrombie and Mr. J. H. Foreshaw in 1943. By the building of their "new towns," the English have characteristically demonstrated that they are not afraid to plan. Also, by preserving barriers of open country (green belts) separating major centers, they have insured future generations against the megalopolis pattern which we experience in the United States when cities merge. There have been mistakes, of course, but by and large our own city governments could learn from the British that planning must be co-ordinated and courageously applied. It must be emphasized, however, that using the English plans as a model is a matter of policy, not practice, for their plans would not in any case be applicable to America. Ours is a very different culture.

No plan is perfect, yet plans are necessary if we are to avoid complete chaos. Because environment structures relationships and planners cannot think of everything, important features will inevitably be omitted. To reduce the serious human consequences of planning errors, there must be built-in research programs which are adequately staffed and soundly financed. Such research is no more a luxury than are the gauges in an airplane cockpit.

XIV

PROXEMICS AND THE FUTURE OF MAN

This book emphasizes that virtually everything that man is and does is associated with the experience of space. Man's sense of space is a synthesis of many sensory inputs: visual, auditory, kinesthetic, olfactory, and thermal. Not only does each of these constitute a complex system—as, for example, the dozen different ways of experiencing depth visually—but each is molded and patterned by culture. Hence, there is no alternative to accepting the fact that people reared in different cultures live in different sensory worlds.

We learn from the study of culture that the patterning of perceptual worlds is a function not only of culture but of *relationship, activity,* and *emotion.* Therefore, people from different cultures, when interpreting each other's behavior, often misinterpret the relationship, the activity, or the emotions. This leads to alienation in encounters or distorted communications.

The study of culture in the proxemic sense is therefore the study of people's use of their sensory apparatus in different emotional states during different activities, in different relationships, and in different settings and contexts. No single research technique is sufficient in scope to investigate a complex, multidimensional subject like proxemics. The technique employed is a function of the particular facet of proxemics under examination at a given moment. In general, however, in the course of my research I have been more concerned with structure than content and more interested in the question "How?" than "Why?"

FORM *vs.* FUNCTION, CONTENT *vs.* STRUCTURE

To ask questions which are addressed to form *vs.* function such as, "Do we grasp because we have hands or do we have hands because we grasp?" has proved quite fruitless in my opinion. I have not been as preoccupied with the content of culture as some of my colleagues, for it has been my experience that overemphasis on content often results in distortion. It also leads to failure to understand situations where content has been greatly diminished. This is the case with American Negro culture, for example. In fact, it is believed by many that American Negroes have no culture of their own simply because the visibly explicit content of their culture has been reduced. For such observers, the Spanish American in New Mexico who speaks English, sends his children to an urban school, lives in a modern house, and drives a Buick, has the same culture as his Anglo-American neighbors. While I take exception to this point of view, it has, in fact, been slowly changing, witness Glazer and Moynihan's book, *Beyond the Melting Pot.* The point I wish to make is subtle and offers many opportunities for misunderstanding. This is because I have generalized about groups that are clearly distinguishable from each other in some contexts (for the most part in their private life), and indistinguishable in others (predominantly in their public life), or where content is quite similar but structure varies. As the reader might suspect, proxemic patterns are only a few of the many differences that do enable people to distinguish one group from another.

For example, I have recently been conducting research on non-verbal communication between lower-class Negroes and lower middle-class whites. Differences in the handling of time represent a very common source of misunderstanding. In addition, the voice, the feet, hands, eyes, body, and space are all handled differently, which often causes even highly motivated Negroes to fail to get jobs for which they apply. These failures are not always because of prejudice, but can be traced to instances where both parties misread each other's behavior. In general, the Negro communications which my students and I have been studying tend to be quite subtle so that even the signs reflecting the strength of the Negro's desire for a particular job may go undetected by the white interviewers who are looking for strong motivation as an important indicator that the applicant would do well. At times like these one can demonstrate the danger of overemphasizing content. The Negro is well aware of the fact that his white interlocutor is not "reading him." What he doesn't know is that while he may be more aware of the nuances of white-Negro interaction than the white man, there are many, many points at which he too is being miscued.

Because we Americans apparently direct our attention more toward content than structure or form, the importance of culture is often minimized. We tend to overlook the influence of the form of a building on the people in it, or the results of overcrowding on Negroes, or the consequences of having one's senses conditioned by Negro culture while trying to cope with "white" teachers and "white" educational materials. *Most important, we have consistently failed to accept the reality of different cultures within our national boundaries.* Negroes, Indians, Spanish Americans, and Puerto Ricans are treated as though they were recalcitrant, undereducated, middle-class Americans of northern European heritage instead of what they really are: members of culturally differentiated enclaves with their own communication systems, institutions, and values. Because we Americans have an "a-cultural bias" we believe only in the superficial differences between the peoples of the world. Not only do we miss much of the richness which comes from knowing others but often we are slow to correct our actions when difficulties begin to develop. Instead of pausing and taking a second look, we are apt to increase our earlier efforts, which can have serious, often unexpected consequences. Furthermore, preoccupation with the content of communications often blinds us to the adumbrative or foreshadowing functions of communication referred to in Chapter I. When people don't respond to adumbrative communications, emotional commitment moves from out-of-awareness to increasingly higher levels of awareness. It is at the point at which the ego is consciously involved that it is difficult to back out of a controversy; whereas the ability to correctly assess adumbrative shifts smooths ruffled feathers before one is cognizant that a situation is even developing. In animals terrible fighting breaks out when adumbrative sequences are short-circuited. This happens with overcrowding or when strange animals are introduced into a stable situation.

MAN'S BIOLOGICAL PAST

Western man has set himself apart from nature and, therefore, from the rest of the animal world. He could have continued to ignore the realities of his animal constitution if it had not been for the population explosion, which has become particularly acute in the past twenty years. This, together with the implosion into our cities of poverty-stricken people from rural areas, has created a condition which has all the earmarks of population buildup and subsequent crash in the animal world. Americans in the 1930s and '40s used to fear economic cycles; today we may have more to be alarmed about in the population cycle.

Many ethologists have been reluctant to suggest that their findings apply to man, even though crowded, overstressed animals are known to suffer from circulatory disorders, heart attacks, and lowered resistance to disease. One of the chief differences between man and animals is that man has domesticated himself by developing his extensions and then proceeded to screen his senses so that he could get more people into a smaller space. Screening helps, but the ultimate buildup can still be lethal. The last instance of severe urban overcrowding over a significant period of time was in the Middle Ages, which were punctuated by disastrous plagues.

Harvard historian William Langer, in his article "The Black Death," states that from 1348 to 1350, after a period of rather rapid growth, the population of Europe was reduced one-quarter by the plague. Transmitted by fleas from rats to man, this disease was caused by a specific organism (*Bacillus pestis*). There is little agreement as to why the plague ended, and, while the relationship of man to the disease is certainly complex, there is something suggestive about the fact that the end of the plague coincided with social and architectural changes that must have considerably reduced the stress of urban living. I am referring to the changes in the home described by Philippe Ariès which protected and solidified the family (see Chapter IX). These changed conditions bolstered by more stable political conditions did much to reduce the stress from crowded urban living.

If man does pay attention to animal studies, he can detect the gradually emerging outlines of an endocrine servomechanism not unlike the thermostat in his house. The only difference is that instead of regulating heat the endocrine control system regulates the population. The most significant discoveries of experimental ethologists whose works are described in Chapters II and III are the catastrophic physiological and behavioral consequences of population buildup prior to crash, and the advantages enjoyed by those animals which have a territory, a space of their own.

Recent reports by pathologists H. L. Ratcliffe and R. L. Snyder of the Philadelphia Zoo's Penrose Laboratory may be of interest. Their report on a twenty-five-year cause-of-death study of 16,000 birds and mammals demonstrates not only that a wide variety of animals are stressed from overcrowding but that they suffer from exactly the same diseases as man: high blood pressure, circulatory diseases, and heart disease, even when fed a low-fat diet.

The animal studies also teach us that crowding per se is neither good nor bad, but rather that overstimulation and disruptions of social relationships as a consequence of overlapping personal distances lead to population collapse. Proper screening can reduce both the disruption and the overstimulation, and permits much higher concentrations of populalations. Screening is what we get from rooms, apartments, and buildings in cities. Such screening works until several individuals are crowded into one room; then a drastic change occurs. The walls no longer shield and protect, but instead press inward on the inhabitants.

By domesticating himself, man has greatly reduced the flight distance of his aboriginal state, which is an absolute necessity when population densities are high. The flight reaction (keeping distance between one's self and the enemy) is one of the most basic and successful ways of coping with danger, but there must be sufficient space if it is to function. Through a process of taming, most higher organisms, including man, can be squeezed into a given area provided that they feel safe and their aggressions are under control. However, if men are made fearful of each other, fear resurrects the flight reaction, creating an explosive need for space. Fear, plus crowding, then produces panic.

Failure to appreciate the importance of the intimate relationship of man to his environment has led to tragic consequences in the past. Psychologist Marc Fried and sociologist Chester Hartman reported deep depression and grief on the part of the relocated Boston West Enders following the destruction of their urban village as part of a renewal program. It wasn't just the environment for which the West Enders grieved but the entire complex of relationships—building, streets, and people—as an integrated way of life. Their world had been shattered.

THE NEED FOR ANSWERS

In order to solve the many complex urban problems facing the United States today we must begin by questioning our basic assumptions concerning the relationship of man to his environment, as well as man's relationship to himself. Over two thousand years ago, Plato concluded that the most difficult task in the world was to know one's self. This truth has to be continually rediscovered; its implications are yet to be fully realized.

The discovery of self on the level of culture is possibly even more demanding than it is on the individual level. The difficulty of this task, however, should not cause us to slight its importance. Americans must be willing to underwrite and participate in team research on a massive scale directed toward learning more about the interrelationship of man and his environment. A point repeatedly stressed by the transactional psychologists has been *the error of assuming that these two were separate and not part and parcel of one interacting system* (see Kilpatrick's book, *Explorations in Transactional Psychology*).

In the words of Ian Mc Harg writing in "Man and His Environment" in *The Urban Condition:*

> . . . no species can exist without an environment, no species can exist in an environment of its exclusive creation, no species can survive, save as a non-disruptive member of an ecological community. Every member must adjust to other members of the community and to the environment in order to survive. Man is not excluded from this test.

It isn't just that Americans must be willing to spend the money. Some deeper changes are called for which are difficult to define, such as a rekindling of the adventuresome spirit and excitement of our frontier days. For we are confronted with urban and cultural frontiers today. The question is, How can we develop them? Our past history of anti-intellectualism is costing us dearly, for the wilderness we must now master is one requiring brains rather than brawn. We need both excitement and ideas and we will discover that both are more apt to be found in people than in things, in structure than content, in involvement rather than in detachment from life.

Anthropologists and psychologists must discover how to compute peoples' involvement ratios in a reasonably simple way. It is known, for example, that some groups, such as the Italians and Greeks, are much more sensorially involved with each other than some other groups, such as the Germans and the Scandinavians. In order to plan intelligently we must have a quantitative measure of such involvement. Once we know how to compute involvement ratios, questions for which we will need answers are: What is maximum, minimum, and ideal density for rural, urban, and transition groups? What is the maximum viable size of the different groups living under urban conditions before normal social controls begin to break down? What different types of small communities are there? How related do they need to be? How are they integrated into larger wholes? In other words, how many different urban biotopes are there? Is the number unlimited or is it possible to categorize them? How can space be used therapeutically to help relieve social tensions and cure social ills?

YOU CAN'T SHED CULTURE

In the briefest possible sense, the message of this book is that no matter how hard man tries it is impossible for him to divest himself of his own culture, for it has penetrated to the roots of his nervous system and determines how he perceives the world. Most of culture lies hidden and is outside voluntary control, making up the warp and weft of human existence. Even when small fragments of culture are elevated to awareness, they are difficult to change, not only because they are so personally experienced but *because people cannot act or interact at all in any meaningful way except through the medium of culture.*

Man and his extensions constitute one interrelated system. It is a mistake of the greatest magnitude to act as though man were one thing and his house or his cities, his technology or his language were something else. Because of the interrelationship between man and his extensions, it behooves us to pay much more attention to what kinds of extensions we create, not only for ourselves but for others for whom they may be ill suited. The relationship of man to his extensions is simply a continuation and a specialized form of the relationship of organisms in general to their environment. However, when an organ or process becomes extended, evolution speeds up at such a rate that it is possible for the extension to take over. This is what we see in our cities and in automation. This is what Norbert Wiener was talking about when he foresaw dangers in the computer, a specialized extension of part of man's brain. Because extensions are numb (and often dumb, as well), it is necessary to build feedback (research) into them so that we can know what is happening, particularly in regard to extensions that mold or substitute for the natural environment. This feedback must be strengthened both in our cities and in our conduct of interethnic relations.

The ethnic crisis, the urban crisis, and the education crisis are interrelated. If viewed comprehensively all three can be seen as different facets of a larger crisis, a natural outgrowth of man's having developed a new dimension—*the cultural dimension*—most of which is hidden from view. The question is, How long can man afford to consciously ignore his own dimension?

APPENDIX

SUMMARY OF JAMES GIBSON'S
THIRTEEN VARIETIES OF PERSPECTIVE
AS ABSTRACTED FROM
THE PERCEPTION OF THE VISUAL WORLD

In the beginning of his book, Gibson says that there is no such thing as perception of space without a *continuous* background surface. Also, like the transactional psychologists, he observes that perception depends upon memory or past stimulation, i.e., it has a *past* that lays the foundation for the perceptions of here and how. He identifies thirteen varieties of perspective "sensory shifts"—visual impressions which accompany the perceptions of depth over a continuous surface and "depth at a contour." These sensory shifts and varieties of perspective are somewhat analogous to the large classes of the contrasting sounds that we call vowels and consonants. They constitute the basic structural categories of experience into which the more specific varieties of vision fit. In other words, a scene contains *information* that is built up out of a number of different elements. What Gibson has done is to analyze and describe the system and the component "stimulus variables" which combine to provide the information man needs in order to move about effectively and to do all that movement implies on the surface of our globe. The important thing is that Gibson has given us a complete system and not just unrelated parts of a system.

Gibson's sensory shift and varieties of perspective fall into four classes: perspective of position; perspective of parallax;

perspective independent of position or motion; and depth at a contour.

Many of these will be readily recognized by the reader. Their importance and the significance of their description is evidenced by the talent, energy, and emotion that have gone into the many different attempts on the part of painters to discover and describe these same principles. Spengler recognized this when he characterized spatial awareness as the prime symbol of Western culture. Writers like Conrad, who wanted to make his readers see what he had seen, and Melville, who was obsessed with communication, built and continue to build their visual imagery on the process described below.

A. *Perspectives of Position*

1. TEXTURE PERSPECTIVE. This is the gradual increase in the density of the texture of a surface as it recedes in the distance.

2. SIZE PERSPECTIVE. As the objects get farther away they decrease in size. (Apparently not fully recognized by the Italian painters in the twelfth century as applying to humans.)

3. LINEAR PERSPECTIVE. Possibly the most commonly known form of perspective in the Western world. Renaissance art is the best known for its incorporation of the so-called laws of perspective. Parallel lines like railroad tracks or highways that join at a single vanishing point at the horizon illustrate this form of perspective.

B. *Perspectives of Parallax*

4. BINOCULAR PERSPECTIVE. Binocular perspective operates very much out of awareness. It is sensed because, owing to the separation of the eyes, each projects a different image. The difference is much more apparent at close distances than at great distances. Closing and opening one eye and then the other makes the differences in the images apparent.

5. MOTION PERSPECTIVE. As one moves forward in space, the closer one approaches a stationary object, the faster it appears to move. Likewise, objects moving at uniform speeds appear to be moving more slowly as distance increases.

C. *Perspectives Independent of the Position or Motion of the Observer*

6. AERIAL PERSPECTIVE. Western ranchers used to have fun at the expense of dudes unfamiliar with regional differences in "aerial perspective." Untold numbers of these innocents would awaken refreshed and stimulated, look out the window and, seeing what looked like a nearby hill, announce that it was such a nice, clear morning they were going to walk to the hill and back before breakfast. Some were dissuaded. Others took off only to discover that the hill was little closer at the end of half an hour's walk than when they started. The "hill" proved to be a mountain anywhere from three to seven miles away and was seen in reduced scale because of an unfamiliar form of aerial perspective. The extreme clarity of the dry, high-altitude air altered the aerial perspective, giving the impression that everything was miles closer than it really was. From this we gather that aerial perspective is derived from the increased haziness and *changes in color* due to the intervening atmosphere. It is an indicator of distance but not as stable and reliable as some of the other forms of perspective.

7. THE PERSPECTIVE OF BLUR. Photographers and painters are more likely than laymen to be aware of perspective of blur. This form of visual space perception is evident when focusing on an object held out in front of the face, so that the background is blurred. Objects in a visual plane other than the one on which the eyes are focused will be seen less distinctly.

8. RELATIVE UPWARD LOCATION IN THE VISUAL FIELD. On the deck of a ship or on the plains of Kansas and eastern Colorado, the horizon is seen as a line at about eye level. The surface of the globe climbs, as it were, from one's feet to eye level. The further from the ground one is, the more pronounced this effect. In the context of everyday experience, one looks *down* at objects that are close and *up* to objects that are far away.

9. SHIFT OF TEXTURE OR LINEAR SPACING. A valley seen

over the edge of a cliff is perceived as more distant because of the break or rapid increase in texture density. Although several years have passed since I first saw a certain Swiss valley, I can recall clearly the bizarre sensations it produced. Standing on a grassy ledge, I looked down 1500 feet at the streets and houses of a village. Blades of grass were sharply etched in the visual field, while each blade was the width of one of the small houses.

10. SHIFT IN THE AMOUNT OF DOUBLE IMAGERY. If one looks at a distant point, everything between the viewer and the point will be seen as double. The closer to the viewer, the greater the doubling; the more distant the point, the less doubling. The gradient in the shift is a cue to distance; a steep gradient is read as close, a gradual gradient as far.

11. SHIFT IN THE RATE OF MOTION. One of the most dependable and consistent ways of sensing depth is the differential movement of objects in the visual field. Those objects which are close move much more than distant objects. They also move more quickly, as noted in Point 5. If two objects are seen as overlapping and they do not shift positions relative to each other when the viewer changes positions, they are either on the same plane or so far away that the shift is not perceived. Television audiences have become accustomed to perspective of this type because it is so pronounced whenever the camera moves through space in a manner similar to the moving viewer.

12. COMPLETENESS OR CONTUNUITY OF OUTLINE. One feature of depth perception that has been exploited during wartime is *continuity of outline*. Camouflage is deceptive because it breaks the continuity. Even if there is no texture difference, no shift in double imagery, and no shift in the rate of motion, the manner in which one object obscures (eclipses) another determines whether the one is seen as behind the other or not. If, for example, the *outline* of the nearest object is unbroken and that of the obscured objects is broken in the process of being eclipsed, this fact will cause one object to appear behind the other.

13. TRANSITIONS BETWEEN LIGHT AND SHADE. Just as an abrupt shift or change in the texture of an object in the

visual field will signal a cliff or an edge, so will an abrupt shift in *brightness* be interpreted as an edge. Gradual transitions in brightness are the principal means of perceiving molding or roundness.

BIBLIOGRAPHY AND REFERENCES

ALLEE, WARDER C. *The Social Life of Animals.* Boston: Beacon Press, 1958.

AMES, ADELBERT. *See* Kilpatrick.

APPLEYARD, DONALD, LYNCH, KEVIN, and MYER, JOHN R. *The View from the Road.* Cambridge: The MIT Press and Harvard University Press, 1963.

ARIÈS, PHILIPPE. *Centuries of Childhood.* New York: Alfred A. Knopf, 1962.

AUDEN, W. H. "Prologue: The Birth of Architecture." *About the House.* New York: Random House, 1965.

BAIN, A. D. "Dominance in the Great Tit, Parus Major." *Scottish Naturalist,* Vol. 61 (1949), pp. 369–472.

BAKER, A., DAVIES, R. L., and SIVADON, P. *Psychiatric Services and Architecture.* Geneva: World Health Organization, 1959.

BALINT, MICHAEL. "Friendly Expanses—Horrid Empty Spaces." *International Journal of Psychoanalysis,* 1945.

BARKER, ROGER G., and WRIGHT, HERBERT F. *Midwest and Its Children.* Evanston: Row, Peterson & Company, 1954.

BARNES, ROBERT D. "Thermography of the Human Body." *Science,* Vol. 140 (May 24, 1963), pp. 870–77.

BATESON, GREGORY. "Minimal Requirements for a Theory of Schizophrenia." *AMA Archives General Psychiatry,* Vol. 2 (1960), pp. 477–91.

BATESON, GREGORY, with JACKSON, D. D., HALEY, J., and WEAKLAND, J. H. "Toward a Theory of Schizophrenia." *Behavioral Science,* Vol. 1 (1956), pp. 251–64.

For description of Bateson's work and discussion of his term "double bind" see chapter by Don D. Jackson, "Interactional Psychotherapy," in *Contemporary Psychotherapies*, edited by Morris I. Stein. New York: Free Press of Glencoe, 1961.

BENEDICT, RUTH. *Chrysanthemum and the Sword.* Boston: Houghton Mifflin, 1946.

BERKELEY, GEORGE (Bishop Berkeley). *A New Theory of Vision and Other Writings.* (Everyman's Library edition) New York: E. P. Dutton, 1922.

BIRDWHISTELL, RAYMOND, L. *Introduction to Kinesics.* Louisville: University of Louisville Press, 1952.

BLACK, JOHN W. "The Effect of Room Characteristics upon Vocal Intensity and Rate." *Journal of Acoustical Society of America,* Vol. 22 (March 1950), pp. 174–76.

BLOOMFIELD, LEONARD. *Language.* New York: H. Holt & Company, 1933.

BOAS, FRANZ. Introduction, *Handbook of American Indian Languages.* Bureau of American Ethnology Bulletin 40. Washington, D.C.: Smithsonian Institution, 1911.

—— *The Mind of Primitive Man.* New York: The Macmillan Company, 1938.

BOGARDUS, E. S. *Social Distance.* Yellow Springs, Ohio: Antioch Press, 1959.

BONNER, JOHN T. "How Slime Molds Communicate." *Scientific American,* Vol. 209, No. 2 (August 1963), pp. 84–86.

BRODEY, WARREN. "Sound and Space." *Journal of the American Institute of Architects,* Vol. 42, No. 1 (July 1964), pp. 58–60.

BRUNER, JEROME. *The Process of Education.* Cambridge: Harvard University Press, 1959.

BUTLER, SAMUEL. *The Way of All Flesh.* Garden City, N.Y.: Doubleday & Company, Inc.

CALHOON, S. W., and LUMLEY, F. H. "Memory Span for Words Presented Auditorially." *Journal of Applied Psychology,* Vol. 18 (1934), pp. 773–84.

CALHOUN, JOHN B. "A 'Behavioral Sink,'" in Eugene L. Bliss, ed., *Roots of Behavior.* New York: Harper & Brothers, 1962. Ch. 22.

—— "Population Density and Social Pathology." *Scientific American,* Vol. 206 (February 1962), pp. 139–46.

—— "The Study of Wild Animals under Controlled Condi-

tions." *Annals of the New York Academy of Sciences,*
Vol. 51 (1950), pp. 113–22.

CANTRIL, HADLEY. *See* Kilpatrick.

CARPENTER, C. R. "Territoriality: A Review of Concepts and
Problems," in A. Roe and G. G. Simpson, eds., *Behavior
and Evolution.* New Haven: Yale University Press, 1958.

CARPENTER, EDMUND, VARLEY, FREDERICK, and FLAHERTY,
ROBERT. *Eskimo.* Toronto: University of Toronto Press,
1959.

CHOMBART DE LAUWE, PAUL. *Famille et Habitation.* Paris:
Editions du Centre National de la Recherche Scientific,
1959.

—— "Le Milieu Social et L'Etude Sociologique des Cas In-
dividuels." *Informations Sociales,* Paris, Vol. 2 (1959),
pp. 41–54.

CHRISTIAN, JOHN J. "The Pathology of Overpopulation." *Military Medicine,* Vol. 128, No. 7 (July 1963), pp. 571–603.

CHRISTIAN, JOHN J., and DAVIS, DAVID E. "Social and Endocrine Factors Are Integrated in the Regulation of Growth
of Mammalian Populations." *Science,* Vol. 146 (December
18, 1964), pp. 1550–60.

CHRISTIAN, JOHN J., with FLYGER, VAGN, and DAVIS, DAVID
E. "Phenomena Associated with Population Density." *Proceedings National Academy of Science,* Vol. 47 (1961),
pp. 428–49.

—— "Factors in Mass Mortality of a Herd of Sika Deer
(*Cervus nippon*)." *Chesapeake Science,* Vol. 1, No. 2
(June 1960), pp. 79–95.

DEEVEY, EDWARD S. "The Hare and the Haruspex: A Cautionary Tale," *Yale Review,* Winter 1960.

DE GRAZIA, SEBASTIAN. *Of Time, Work, and Leisure.* New
York: Twentieth Century, 1962.

DELOS SECRETARIAT. "Report of the Second Symposion."
Delos Secretariat, Athens Center of Ekistics, Athens,
Greece (*See* Watterson).

DORNER, ALEXANDER. *The Way Beyond Art.* New York: New
York University Press, 1958.

DOXIADIS, CONSTANTINOS A. *Architecture in Transition.* New
York: Oxford University Press, 1963.

EIBL-EIBESFELDT, I. "The Fighting Behavior of Animals."

Scientific American, Vol. 205, No. 6 (December 1961), pp. 112–22.

EINSTEIN, ALBERT. Foreword, *Concepts of Space* by Max Jammer. New York: Harper Torch Books, 1960.

ERRINGTON, PAUL. *Muskrats and Marsh Management.* Harrisburg: Stackpole Company, 1961.

—— *Of Men and Marshes.* New York: The Macmillan Company, 1957.

—— "Factors Limiting Higher Vertebrate Populations." *Science,* Vol. 124 (August 17, 1956), pp. 304–07.

—— "The Great Horned Owl as an Indicator of Vulnerability in the Prey Populations." *Journal of Wild Life Management,* Vol. 2 (1938).

FRANK, LAWRENCE K. "Tactile Communications." *ETC. A Review of General Semantics,* Vol. 16 (1958), pp. 31–97.

FRIED, MARC. "Grieving for a Lost Home," in Leonard J. Duhl, ed., *The Urban Condition.* New York: Basic Books, 1963.

FRIED, MARC, with GLEICHER, PEGGY. "Some Sources of Residential Satisfaction in an Urban Slum." *Journal of the American Institute of Planners,* Vol. 27 (1961).

FULLER, R. BUCKMINSTER. *Education Automation.* Carbondale: Southern Illinois University Press, 1963.

—— *No More Secondhand God.* Carbondale: Southern Illinois University Press, 1963.

—— *Ideas and Integrities.* Englewood Cliffs, N.J.: Prentice-Hall, 1963.

—— *The Unfinished Epic of Industrialization.* Charlotte: Heritage Press, 1963.

—— *Nine Chains to the Moon.* Carbondale: Southern Illinois University Press, 1963.

GANS, HERBERT. *The Urban Villagers.* Cambridge: The MIT Press and Harvard University Press, 1960.

GAYDOS, H. F. "Intersensory Transfer in the Discrimination of Form." *American Journal of Psychology,* Vol. 69 (1956), pp. 107–10.

GELDARD, FRANK A. "Some Neglected Possibilities of Communication." *Science,* Vol. 131 (May 27, 1960), pp. 1583–88.

GIBSON, JAMES J. *The Perception of the Visual World*. Boston: Houghton Mifflin, 1950.

—— "Observations on Active Touch." *Psychological Review*, Vol. 69, No. 6 (November 1962), pp. 477–91.

—— "Ecological Optics," *Vision Research*, Vol. 1 (1961), pp. 253–62. Printed in Great Britain by Pergamon Press.

—— "Pictures, Perspective and Perception." *Daedalus*, Winter 1960.

GIEDION, SIGFRIED. *The Eternal Present: The Beginnings of Architecture*, Vol. II. New York: Bollingen Foundation, Pantheon Books, 1962.

GILLIARD, E. THOMAS. "Evolution of Bowerbirds." *Scientific American*, Vol. 209, No. 2 (August 1963), pp. 38–46.

—— "On the Breeding Behavior of the Cock-of-the-Rock (Aves, *Rupicola rupicola*)." *Bulletin of the American Museum of Natural History*, Vol. 124 (1962).

GLAZER, NATHAN, and MOYNIHAN, DANIEL PATRICK. *Beyond the Melting Pot*. Cambridge: The MIT Press and the Harvard University Press, 1963.

GOFFMAN, ERVING. *Behavior in Public Places*. New York: Free Press of Glencoe, 1963.

—— *Encounters*. Indianapolis: Bobbs-Merrill, 1961.

—— *The Presentation of Self in Everyday Life*. Garden City, N.Y.: Doubleday & Company, Inc., 1959.

GOLDFINGER, ERNO. "The Elements of Enclosed Space." *Architectural Review*, January 1942, pp. 5–9.

—— "The Sensation of Space. Urbanism and Spatial Order." *Architectural Review*, November 1941, pp. 129–31.

GROSSER, MAURICE. *The Painter's Eye*. New York: Rinehart & Company, 1951.

GRUEN, VICTOR. *The Heart of Our Cities*. New York: Simon and Schuster, 1964.

GUTKIND, E. H. *The Twilight of Cities*. New York: Free Press of Glencoe, 1962.

HALL, EDWARD T. *The Silent Language*. Garden City, N.Y.: Doubleday & Company, Inc., 1959.

—— "Adumbration in Intercultural Communication." The Ethnography of Communication, Special Issue, *American Anthropologist*, Vol. 66, No. 6, Part II (December 1964), pp. 154–63.

—— "Silent Assumptions in Social Communication." *Disorders of Communication*, Vol. XLII, edited by Rioch and Weinstein. Research Publications, Association for Research in Nervous and Mental Disease, Baltimore: Williams and Wilkins Company, 1964.

—— "A System for the Notation of Proxemic Behavior." *American Anthropologist*, Vol. 65, No. 5 (October 1963), pp. 1003–26.

—— "Proxemics—A Study of Man's Spatial Relationships," in I. Galdston, ed., *Man's Image in Medicine and Anthropology*. New York: International Universities Press, 1963.

—— "Quality in Architecture—An Anthropological View." *Journal of the American Institute of Architects*, July 1963.

—— "The Madding Crowd." *Landscape*, Fall 1962.

—— "The Language of Space." *Landscape*, Fall 1960.

HARTMAN, CHESTER W. "Social Values and Housing Orientations." *Journal of Social Issues*, January 1963.

HEDIGER, H. *Studies of the Psychology and Behavior of Captive Animals in Zoos and Circuses.* London: Butterworth & Company, 1955.

—— *Wild Animals in Captivity.* London: Butterworth & Company, 1950.

—— "The Evolution of Territorial Behavior," in S. L. Washburn, ed., *Social Life of Early Man*. New York: Viking Fund Publications in Anthropology, No. 31 (1961).

HELD, RICHARD, and FREEDMAN, S. J. "Plasticity in Human Sensory Motor Control." *Science*, Vol. 142 (October 25, 1963), pp. 455–62.

HESS, ECKHARD H. "Pupil Size as Related to Interest Value of Visual Stimuli." *Science*, Vol. 132 (1960), pp. 349–50.

HINDE, R. A., and TINBERGEN, NIKO. "The Comparative Study of Species—Specific Behavior," in A. Roe and G. G. Simpson, eds., *Behavior and Evolution*. New Haven: Yale University Press, 1958.

HOCKETT, CHARLES F., and ASHER, ROBERT. "The Human Revolution." *Current Anthropology*, Vol. 5, No. 3 (June 1964).

HOWARD, H. E. *Territory in Bird Life*. London: Murray, 1920.

HUGHES, RICHARD. *A High Wind in Jamaica.* New York: New American Library, 1961.

ITTELSON, WILLIAM H. *See* Kilpatrick.

IZUMI, K. "An Analysis for the Design of Hospital Quarters for the Neuropsychiatric Patient." *Mental Hospitals* (Architectural Supplement), April 1957.

JACOBS, JANE. *The Death and Life of Great American Cities.* New York: Random House, 1961.

JOOS, MARTIN. "The Five Clocks." *International Journal American Linguistics,* April 1962.

KAFKA, FRANZ. *The Trial.* New York: Alfred A. Knopf, 1948.

KAWABATA, YASUNARI. *Snow Country.* New York: Alfred A. Knopf, 1957.

KEENE, DONALD. *Living Japan.* Garden City, N.Y.: Doubleday & Company, Inc., 1959.

KEPES, GYORGY. *The Language of Vision.* Chicago: Paul Theobald, 1944.

KILPATRICK, F. P. *Explorations in Transactional Psychology.* New York: New York University Press, 1961. Contains articles by *Adelbert Ames, Hadley Cantril, William Ittelson, F. P. Kilpatrick,* and other transactional psychologists.

KLING, VINCENT. "Space: A Fundamental Concept in Design," in C. Goshen, ed., *Psychiatric Architecture.* Washington, D.C.: American Psychiatric Association, 1959.

KROEBER, ALFRED. *An Anthropologist Looks at History,* edited by Theodora Kroeber. Berkeley: University of California Press, 1963.

LA BARRE, WESTON. *The Human Animal.* Chicago: University of Chicago Press, 1954.

LANGER, WILLIAM L. "The Black Death." *Scientific American,* Vol. 210, No. 2 (February 1964), pp. 114–21.

LEONTIEV, A. N. "Problems of Mental Development." Moscow, USSR: RSFSR Academy of Pedagogical Sciences, 1959. (*Psychological Abstracts,* Vol. 36, p. 786.)

LEWIN, KURT, LIPPIT, RONALD, and WHITE, RALPH K. "Patterns of Aggressive Behavior in Experimentally Created 'Social Climates.'" *Journal of Social Psychology,* SPSSI Bulletin, Vol. 10 (1939), pp. 271–99.

LISSMAN, H. W. "Electric Location by Fishes." *Scientific American*, Vol. 208, No. 3 (March 1963), pp. 50–59.

LONDON COUNTY COUNCIL. *Administrative County of London Development Plan. First Review 1960*. London: The London County Council, 1960.

LORENZ, KONRAD. *Das Sogenannte Böse; Zur Naturgeschichte der Aggression*. (The biology of aggression.) Vienna: Dr. G. Borotha-Schoeler Verlag, 1964.

—— *Man Meets Dog*. Cambridge: Riverside Press, 1955.

—— *King Solomon's Ring*. New York: Crowell, 1952.

—— "The Role of Aggression in Group Formation," in Schaffner, ed., *Group Process*. Transactions of the fourth conference sponsored by Josiah Macy, Jr., Foundation. Princeton: 1957.

LYNCH, KEVIN. *The Image of the City*. Cambridge: The MIT Press and Harvard University Press, 1960.

MCBRIDE, GLEN. *A General Theory of Social Organization and Behavior*. St. Lucia, Australia: University of Queensland Press, 1964.

MCCULLOCH, WARREN S. "Teleological Mechanisms." *Annals of the New York Academy of Sciences*, Vol. 50, Art. 9 (1948).

MCCULLOCH, WARREN S., and PITTS, WALTER. "How We Know Universals, the Perception of Auditory and Visual Forms." *Bulletin of Mathematical Biophysics*, Vol. 9 (1947), pp. 127–47.

MC HARG, IAN. "Man and His Environment," in Leonard J. Duhl, ed., *The Urban Condition*. New York: Basic Books, 1963.

MCLUHAN, MARSHALL. *Understanding Media*. New York: McGraw-Hill, 1964.

—— *The Gutenberg Galaxy*. Toronto: University of Toronto Press, 1963.

MATORÉ, GEORGES. *L'Espace Humain. L'expression de l'espace dans la vie, la pensée et l'art contemporains*. Paris: Editions La Colombe, 1961.

MEAD, MARGARET, and METRAUX, RHODA. *The Study of Culture at a Distance*. Chicago: University of Chicago Press, 1953.

MOHOLY-NAGY, LASZLO. *The New Vision.* New York: Wittenborn, Schultz, 1949.

MONTAGU, ASHLEY. *The Science of Man.* New York: Odyssey Press, 1964.

MOWAT, FARLEY. *Never Cry Wolf.* Boston: Atlantic Monthly Press. Little, Brown, 1963.

MUMFORD, LEWIS. *The City in History.* New York: Harcourt, Brace, 1961.

NORTHRUP, F. S. C. *Philosophical Anthropology and Practical Politics.* New York: The Macmillan Company, 1960.

OSMOND, HUMPHRY. "The Relationship Between Architect and Psychiatrist," in C. Goshen, ed., *Psychiatric Architecture.* Washington, D.C.: American Psychiatric Association, 1959.

—— "The Historical and Sociological Development of Mental Hospitals," in C. Goshen, ed., *Psychiatric Architecture.* Washington, D.C.: American Psychiatric Association, 1959.

—— "Function as the Basis of Psychiatric Ward Design." *Mental Hospitals* (Architectural Supplement), April 1957, pp. 23–29.

PARKES, A. S., and BRUCE, H. M. "Olfactory Stimuli in Mammalian Reproduction." *Science,* Vol. 134 (October 13, 1961), pp. 1049–54.

PIAGET, JEAN, and INHELDER, BARBEL. *The Child's Concept of Space.* London: Routledge & Kegan Paul, 1956.

PORTMANN, ADOLF. *Animal Camouflage.* Ann Arbor: University of Michigan Press, 1959.

RATCLIFFE, H. L., and SNYDER, ROBERT L. "Patterns of Disease, Controlled Populations, and Experimental Design." *Circulation,* Vol. XXVI (December 1962), pp. 1352–57.

REDFIELD, ROBERT, and SINGER, MILTON. "The Cultural Role of Cities," in Margaret Park Redfield, ed., *Human Nature and the Study of Society,* Vol. 1. Chicago: University of Chicago Press, 1962.

RICHARDSON, JOHN. "Braque Discusses His Art." *Realités,* August 1958, pp. 24–31.

ROSENBLITH, WALTER A. *Sensory Communication.* New York: The MIT Press and John Wiley & Sons, 1961.

ST.-EXUPÉRY, ANTOINE DE. *Flight to Arras.* New York: Reynal and Hitchcock, 1942.

—— *Night Flight.* New York: Century Printing Company, 1932.

SAPIR, EDWARD. *Selected Writings of Edward Sapir in Language, Culture and Personality.* Berkeley: University of California Press, 1949.

—— "The Status of Linguistics as a Science." *Language,* Vol. 5 (1929), pp. 209–10.

SCHÄFER, WILHELM. *Der kritische Raum und die kritische Situation in der tierischen Sozietät.* Frankfurt: Krämer, 1956.

SEARLES, HAROLD. *The Non-Human Environment.* New York: International Universities Press, 1960.

SEBEOK, T. "Evolution of Signaling Behavior." *Behavioral Science,* July 1962, pp. 430–42.

SELYE, HANS. *The Stress of Life.* New York: McGraw-Hill, 1956.

SHOEMAKER, H. "Social Hierarchy in Flocks of the Canary." *The Auk,* Vol. 56: pp. 381–406.

SINGER, MILTON. "The Social Organization of Indian Civilization." *Diogenes,* Spring 1964.

SMITH, CHLOETHIEL W. "Space." *Architectural Forum,* November 1948.

SMITH, KATHLEEN, and SINES, JACOB O. "Demonstration of a Peculiar Odor in the Sweat of Schizophrenic Patients." *AMA Archives of General Psychiatry,* Vol. 2 (February 1960), pp. 184–88.

SNOW, CHARLES PERCY. *The Two Cultures and the Scientific Revolution.* Cambridge, England: Cambridge University Press, 1959.

SNYDER, ROBERT. "Evolution and Integration of Mechanisms that Regulate Population Growth." *National Academy of Sciences,* Vol. 47 (April 1961), pp. 449–55.

SOMMER, ROBERT. "The Distance for Comfortable Conversation: A Further Study." *Sociometry,* Vol. 25 (1962).

—— "Leadership and Group Geography." *Sociometry,* Vol. 24 (1961).

—— "Studies in Personal Space," *Sociometry,* Vol. 22 (1959).

SOMMER, ROBERT, and ROSS, H. "Social Interaction on a Geriatric Ward." *International Journal of Social Psychology*, Vol. 4 (1958), pp. 128–33.

SOMMER, ROBERT, and WHITNEY, G. "Design for Friendship." *Canadian Architect*, 1961.

SOUTHWICK, CHARLES H. "Peromyscus leucopus: An Interesting Subject for Studies of Socially Induced Stress Responses." *Science*, Vol. 143 (January 1964), pp. 55–56.

SPENGLER, OSWALD. *The Decline of the West.* 2 vols. New York: Alfred A. Knopf, 1944.

THIEL, PHILIP. "A Sequence-Experience Notation for Architectural and Urban Space." *Town Planning Review*, April 1961, pp. 33–52.

THOREAU, HENRY DAVID. *Walden.* New York: The Macmillan Company, 1929.

Time MAGAZINE. "No Place Like Home," July 31, 1964, pp. 11–18.

TINBERGEN, NIKO. *Curious Naturalists.* New York: Basic Books, 1958.

—— "The Curious Behavior of the Stickleback." *Scientific American*, Vol. 187, No. 6 (December 1952), pp. 22–26.

TRAGER, GEORGE L., and BLOCH, BERNARD. *Outline of Linguistic Analysis.* Baltimore: Linguistic Society of America, 1942.

TRAGER, GEORGE L., and SMITH, HENRY LEE, JR. *An Outline of English Structure.* Norman: Battenburg Press, 1951.

TWAIN, MARK (SAMUEL L. CLEMENS). "Captain Stormfield's Visit to Heaven," in Charles Neider, ed., *The Complete Mark Twain.* New York: Bantam Books, 1958.

WARD, BARBARA. "The Menace of Urban Explosion." *The Listener*, Vol. 70, No. 1807 (November 14, 1963), pp. 785–87. London: British Broadcasting Corporation.

WATTERSON, JOSEPH. "Delos II. The Second Symposion to Explore the Problems of Human Settlements." *Journal of the American Institute of Architects*, March 1965, pp. 47–53.

WEAKLAND, J. H., and JACKSON, D. D. "Patient and Therapist Observations on the Circumstances of a Schizophrenic Episode." *AMA Archives Neurology and Psychiatry*, Vol. 79 (1958), pp. 554–75.

WHITE, THEODORE H. *The Making of the President 1960.* New York: Atheneum, 1961.

WHITEHEAD, ALFRED NORTH. *Adventures of Ideas.* New York: The Macmillan Company, 1933.

WHORF, BENJAMIN LEE. *Language, Thought, and Reality.* New York: The Technology Press and John Wiley & Sons, 1956.

—— "Linguistic Factors in the Terminology of Hopi Architecture." *International Journal of American Linguistics,* Vol. 19, No. 2 (April 1953).

—— "Science and Linguistics." *The Technology Review,* Vol. XLII, No. 6 (April 1940).

WIENER, NORBERT. *Cybernetics.* New York: John Wiley & Sons, 1948.

—— "Some Moral and Technical Consequences of Automation." *Science,* Vol. 131 (May 6, 1960), pp. 1355–59.

WYNNE-EDWARDS, V. C. *Animal Dispersion in Relation to Social Behavior.* New York: Hafner Publishing Company, 1962.

—— "Self-Regulatory Systems in Populations of Animals." *Science,* Vol. 147 (March 1965), pp. 1543–48.

ZUBEK, JOHN P., and WILGOSH, L. "Prolonged Immobilization of the Body Changes in Performance and in Electroencephalograms." *Science,* Vol. 140 (April 19, 1963), pp. 306–08.

INDEX

EDWARD T. HALL is a widely traveled anthropologist whose field-
work has taken him all over the world—from the Pueblo cultures
of the American Southwest to Europe and the Middle East. As
director of the State Department's Point Four Training Program in
the 1950s, Dr. Hall's mission was to teach foreign-bound techni-
cians and administrators how to communicate effectively across
cultural boundaries. He is a consultant to architects on human
factors in design and to business and government agencies in the
field of intercultural relations, and has taught at the University of
Denver, Bennington College, the Washington School of Psychiatry, the Harvard Business School, the Illinois Institute of Technology, and Northwestern University.

Dr. Hall was born in Webster Groves, Missouri. He received an
A.B. degree from the University of Denver, and M.A. from the
University of Arizona, and a Ph.D. in anthropology from Columbia
University. Part of the year he lives in Santa Fe, New Mexico,
where he writes and does research.